Key Stage 2

ASSESSING
SCIENCE

Neil Burton
with Janet Machin

 **Brilliant Publications**

We hope you and your class enjoy using this book. Other books published by Brilliant Publications include:

If you would like further information on these or other titles published by Brilliant Publications, please write to the address given below.

Published by Brilliant Publications,
1 Church View
Sparrow Hall Farm,
Edlesborough
Dunstable,
Bedfordshire,
LU6 2ES, UK

Tel: 01525 229720
Fax: 01525 229725
E-mail: sales@brilliantpublications.co.uk
Website: www.brilliantpublications.co.uk

The name Brilliant Publications and the logo are registered trademarks.

Written by Neil Burton with Janet Machin
Illustrated by Virginia Grey and Kate Ford
Cover illustration by Virginia Grey

Printed in the UK

First published in 1998. Reprinted 2005.
10 9 8 7 6 5 4 3 2

The right of Neil Burton and Janet Machin to be identified as authors of this work has been asserted by them in accordance with the Copyright, Designs and Patents Act 1988.

© Neil Burton and Janet Machin 1998
ISBN 1 897675 35 6

Contents

Introduction

The aims of the book are twofold:

✳   to encourage the children to think and record their knowledge and understanding in a variety of ways;

✳   to enable teachers to gather evidence from which assessments can be made.

Assessing Science is not a complete scheme of work, but it will supplement and support whatever science scheme is being used. It is designed to be highly compatible with National Curricula throughout the United Kingdom, and that of England and Wales in particular. References relate to the Programmes of Study for the English National Curriculum.

The Qualifications and Assessment Authority (QCA) recommends that judgements regarding level descriptions are made as a result of an accumulation of work. The completed sheets provide a useful record and can be kept and used (along with other work) as a basis for assessing the children's level of attainment.

It is important to ensure that the targets set for the children are sufficiently challenging to allow the children to demonstrate their abilities. It is not uncommon for children to be given a teacher assessment lower than might be expected – not though, due to a lack of ability, but because of a lack of opportunity. Children need to be asked the right question to be able to give the right answer.

Generally, the 'Potential assessment activities' on the teachers' pages give children the opportunity to demonstrate their ability to work in the level description range 2– 5. Each set of activities is designed to be progressively more challenging.

Making best use of the book

The book is structured with teachers' pages and photocopiable masters (PCMs) facing each other. You are strongly recommended to read through the teachers' pages before using the PCMs, to ensure that you choose the sheet that most closely matches the learning objectives you have set for the children.

Teachers' pages
The information is structured under the following headings:

* **National Curriculum focus**
  The National Curriculum references have been written out in full for your convenience.

* **Assessment objective**
  The assessment objective of the PCM is closely linked to the National Curriculum focus.

* **Potential assessment activities**
  Additional, related activities which can be used to assess children's knowledge and understanding.

* **Assessment outcomes**
  These are linked to the 'Potential assessment activities'.

* **Example of a child's response**
  The examples have been typed to make them easier to read. Every child is different but these examples are designed to give a general indication of what might be expected from more able children.

* **Key vocabulary**
  Definitions can be found in the *Teachers' glossary of scientific terms* on pages 94-96.

Photocopiable masters
Some of the PCMs are deliberately open-ended, enabling you to use your professional judgement to provide an appropriate stimulus. Other PCMs offer the opportunity to engage in challenges which will establish the child's level of understanding. Finally there is a selection of sheets, including key making, tabulating and grouping, which focus on particular skills within particular contexts.

Suggestions are given on some of the teachers' pages of ways of adapting the PCMs to allow for differentiation (eg by deleting certain sections before photocopying). You are encouraged to find your own ways of adapting the sheets further. It is recommended that you make your modifications on a photocopy of the sheet, so as to keep the original sheet intact.

The PCMs can be used:

* before teaching to identify the existing level of understanding of the children in order to match their needs accurately;

* as a support and stimulus for practical work, to help children to structure their thinking;

* after your teaching to assess the children's learning (before and after is often quite enlightening – it will give a very good indication as to the effectiveness of your teaching);

* with a variety of group sizes, from whole class to individuals.

Showing what I understand about a process

National Curriculum focus
Sc1/1a that science is about thinking creatively to try to explain how living and non-living things work, and to establish links between causes and effects;
Sc1/2b consider what sources of information, including first-hand experience and a range of other sources, they will use to answer questions.

Assessment objective
The children should demonstrate their understanding of a particular scientific process.

Potential assessment activities	Assessment outcomes
Through discussion (group or class), children examine a process that has been identified (preferably by them) and attempt to explain how they think it works. They summarize their discussion on the PCM.	The explanations that children give should *at least* be consistent with the available empirical evidence.
On the PCM children write (and draw as appropriate) about how they think some scientific process works (eg evaporation, germination, human respiration, etc).	Children should identify where this information originated from (eg book research, practical investigation, TV, general observation, etc). Children should be able to communicate their ideas effectively.
Using the PCM children design an activity (investigation or observation) to test out their ideas. (This could be done in groups.)	Children should, where appropriate, identify and isolate variables in the design of a practical activity.

Example of a child's response

> I have been thinking about what happens when …
> photosynthesis happens in green plants.

> This is what I think happens:
> Carbon dioxide goes into the leaves from the air through tiny holes. It mixes with a green substance called chlorophyll. When the sun shines on the leaf it gives energy to the chlorophyll which makes the carbon dioxide break up into carbon and oxygen. The oxygen goes back into the air and the carbon is used to make the plant grow bigger.

> The reason I think this is because …
> I know that plants are made up of carbon. When you burn wood you get charcoal. We eat plants to get carbohydrates.

> I could check that I'm right by …
> finding a book about plants in the library and reading what it says about photosynthesis.

Key vocabulary
Dependent upon science content.

Showing what I understand about a process

Name _____ Date _____

I have been thinking about what happens when …

This is what I think happens:

The reason I think this is because …

I could check that I'm right by …

This is what I know about ...

National Curriculum focus

Sc1/1a that science is about thinking creatively to try to explain how living and non-living things work, and to establish links between causes and effects;

Sc1/2b consider what sources of information, including first-hand experience and a range of other sources, they will use to answer questions.

Assessment objective

The children should demonstrate their knowledge of a particular area of science and explain how they have obtained this knowledge.

Potential assessment activities	Assessment outcomes
Children write (and draw as appropriate) on the PCM about the 'important' things they know concerning a particular science topic (eg magnetism, rocks, pond life, etc).	Children should identify relevant important points.
Through discussion (group or class), children identify the information they know about a topic and identify ways in which it could be checked. They use the PCM for recording.	Children should identify where this information originated from (eg book research, practical investigation, TV, general observation, etc).

Example of a child's response

> This is what I know about ... how light travels
> Light comes from a source like the Sun or a bulb. We see light using our eyes. When light hits objects it reflects so that we can see them. Some things reflect light better than others making them look brighter or dimmer.

> I know this because ...
> we have to point a torch at something if we want to see it. It is best to wear bright coloured clothes at night so that it is easier for cars to see you.

> I could check that I'm right by ...
> carrying out a fair test to see which colours reflect light the best. Also to see if the colour of light is important.

Key vocabulary

Dependent upon science content.

This is what I know about …

Name_____ Date _____

This is what I know about …

I know this because …

I could check that I'm right by …

Use this sheet to show what you know about seeds, stretchy sponge or circuits.

Be safe!

National Curriculum focus
Sc1/2e   use simple equipment and materials appropriately and take action to control risks.

Assessment objective
The children should demonstrate their ability to identify and respond appropriately to potential hazards in science activities.

Potential assessment activities	Assessment outcomes
Through discussion (group or class), children explore the potential safety issues surrounding a science activity. They use the PCM for recording.	Children should identify potential hazards. Children should suggest ways in which these hazards may be overcome or avoided.
Children discuss the range of options available, in terms of equipment, materials or working practices, to ensure the safest approach to a practical activity. They use the PCM for recording.	Children should know when to ask for advice.
Children, working in groups, design a practical activity (fair test, observation or specimen collection) focusing on the safety aspects.	Children should, where appropriate, work with due regard for hygiene and the safety of other living things.

Example of a child's response

> The activity is about...
> pond dipping and mini-beast collection.

Things that could be hazardous	How we could control the risks
The place we go pond dipping.	Go to a place that has a warden or one that has safe dipping sites.
The germs that could be in the water.	Wear gloves and wash hands.
Falling in the water.	Don't lean over the water. Use proper nets.
Using equipment that might break or shatter.	Use plastic equipment to collect and store the mini-beasts.
The safe handling of the mini-beasts.	Use pooters or spoons to get them from the nets to the containers.
A safe place to keep the mini-beasts.	Have pond water in the containers and take the mini-beasts back after.

Key vocabulary
Dependent upon science content.

Note
Use *Be Safe!* published by the Association for Science Education to ensure that you are following appropriate safety procedures.

Be safe!

Name_____ Date _____

If you don't think very carefully before you do something, or follow instructions to keep you safe, doing science can be hazardous. Before you do your next activity, think about the things that could be hazardous and how you could make sure you stay safe.

The activity is about …

Things that could be hazardous	How we could control the risks

Tell your teacher how you will make your activity safe.

Word map

National Curriculum focus
Sc1/1a   that science is about thinking creatively to try to explain how living and non-living things work, and to establish links between causes and effects.

Assessment objective
The children should demonstrate their understanding of scientific concepts by identifying appropriate vocabulary connected with a scientific topic and linking it together in a scientifically correct way.

Potential assessment activities	Assessment outcomes
The children structure and record their 'brainstorming' of particular scientific topics or concept areas. The actual scientific content of the word map is the crucial element in determining the level of understanding of the child. You may wish to give the children a list of key terminology and see how they make use of them.	Children should be able to identify the key vocabulary concerned with the topic. Children should identify simple, but relevant links. The links should begin to demonstrate an applied understanding which is scientifically correct.
Give the children an extended list where some of the terms are irrelevant and ask them to make a word map.	Children should select which terms are scientifically appropriate for their word map and should make appropriate links using scientific concepts.
Give the children a basic list and ask them to extend it and then to link the terms by making a word map.	Children should identify more detailed vocabulary and make sensible links. Vocabulary and links should be scientifically correct.
Give the children an incorrectly completed word map for them to correct.	Children should identify the links which are scientifically incorrect, and should use vocabulary and new links which are scientifically correct.

Key vocabulary
Dependent on science content.

Example of a child's response

My words are ...
digestion, food, teeth, saliva, stomach, blood, acid, digestive juices,

Use this box to show that you understand the scientific ideas behind the words.

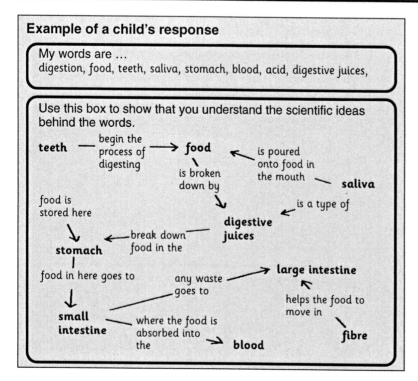

Word map

Name _____ Date_____

Here is my list of important words about …

My words are …

Use this box to show that you understand the scientific ideas behind the words.

Questions

National Curriculum focus
Sc1/2a ask questions that can be investigated scientifically and decide how to find answers.

Assessment objective
The children should demonstrate that they are able to form questions which can be used as the basis of an investigation.

Potential assessment activities	Assessment outcomes
Children structure and record their questions prior to planning a practical scientific activity. For assessment in this area the actual scientific content of the activity is only important insofar as it is relevant to the topic in question.	Children should be able to respond appropriately to suggestions for potential questions in a range of different science contexts.
Children should have the opportunity to put forward their own ideas and ask simple but relevant questions.	Children should identify questions that can be used as the starting points for fair test practical investigations.

Example of a child's response

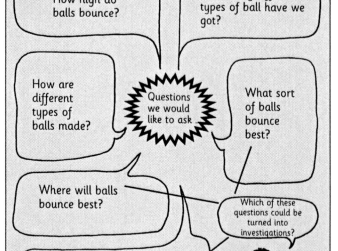

Key vocabulary
Dependent on science content.

Note
Other questions in the 'Example of child's response' might be tackled via surveys (How many different types of ball have we got?); or through research (How are different types of ball made?)

Questions

Name _____ Date _____

We want to find out about …

Questions we would like to ask

Which of these questions could be turned into investigations?

Fair test

National Curriculum focus
Sc1/1b that it is important to test ideas using evidence from observation and measurement;
Sc1/2a ask questions that can be investigated scientifically and decide how to find answers;
Sc1/2c think about what might happen or try things out when deciding what to do, what kind of evidence to collect, and what equipment and materials to use;
Sc1/2d make a fair test or comparison by changing one factor and observing or measuring the effect while keeping other factors the same.

Assessment objective
The children should demonstrate their ability to design a fair test and identify appropriate means of collecting and presenting findings.

Potential assessment activity
Children plan a fair test and consider how the data they might expect to obtain is to be recorded and presented. The PCM should be used in the context of the children carrying out their own practical scientific activity.

Assessment outcome
Children should identify clearly a scientific question that can be answered through investigation or survey, including all of the key factors that might affect the outcome of the investigation. They should know the scale and units of any numerical data that they intend to record and should, where appropriate, choose a suitable means of presenting their data.

Example of a child's response

I am trying to find out...
on which surface the ball bounces best.

I will be changing...
the surfaces that I bounce the ball on.

I will need to observe or measure...
how high the ball bounces. I will drop the ball three times on each surface.
I will use ... a metre stick (units of measurement cm)

I need to keep these things the same each time I do the test:
• the ball I use   • how high I drop it from
• how I measure the bounce

I will record my observations or measurements using...
a table.
surface type | height of bounce

I will present my findings using...
a block chart.
height of bounce
surface type

I will be looking for links between...
how hard or bouncy the surface is and the height the ball bounces to.

Key vocabulary
Dependent on science content.

Fair test

Name _____ Date _____

I am trying to find out …

I will be changing …

I will need to observe or measure …

I will use …   (units of measurement   )

I need to keep these things the same each time I do the test:
-
-
-
-
-
-

I will record my observations or measurements using …

I will present my findings using …

I will be looking for links between …

My plans

National Curriculum focus

Sc1/2a ask questions that can be investigated scientifically and decide how to find answers;

Sc1/2c think about what might happen or try things out when deciding what to do, what kind of evidence to collect, and what equipment and materials to use;

Sc1/2e use simple equipment and materials appropriately and take action to control risks.

Assessment objective

The children should demonstrate that they are able to plan a practical activity in science paying due regard to method, sequence and the choice and use of equipment and materials.

Potential assessment activity	Assessment outcome
Children structure their planning of a fair test and consider how the data they might expect to obtain is to be recorded and presented. In consequence this PCM should be used in the context of children carrying out their own practical scientific activity.	Children should be able to demonstrate their planning abilities in a range of different contexts. They should correctly identify the equipment needed and should be able to describe how to make the investigation/survey more accurate.

Example of a child's response

Key vocabulary
Dependent on science content.

I am trying to find out …
which surface a ball will bounce best on.

This is what I am going to do:

1 I will draw up a results table naming all of the surfaces I am going to use. I will then collect all of the equipment that I will need.

2 I will carry out the fair test making sure that I record all of my results. I will then put all of the things that I have used away.

3 I will present my results on a block chart. I might use the computer to do this using a spreadsheet.

4

I am going to need …
a ball, a metre stick, different surfaces to bounce on (carpet, carpet tiles, tiled floor, wooden floor, playground, lawn, school field, sand tray, PE mats, table top), someone to drop the ball, my results table and a pencil.

To ensure that my findings are accurate I will …
do each test three times, drop the same ball from the same height, measure the bounce to the same part of the ball each time.

My plans

Name _____ Date _____

I am trying to find out …

This is what I am going to do:

1

2

3

4

I am going to need …

To ensure my findings are accurate I will …

What I think now

National Curriculum focus

Sc1/2c think about what might happen or try things out when deciding what to do, what kind of evidence to collect, and what equipment and materials to use;

Sc1/2j use observations, measurements or other data to draw conclusions;

Sc1/2k decide whether these conclusions agree with any prediction made and/or whether they enable further predictions to be made;

Sc1/2l use their scientific knowledge and understanding to explain observations, measurements or other data or conclusions.

Assessment objective

The children should demonstrate their ability to make predictions based upon their scientific understanding and reflect on these ideas after having tested them.

Potential assessment activity	Assessment outcome
Children should be given a topic for investigation. They should make predictions prior to carrying out the investigation and have the opportunity to reflect on their predictions after having tested them.	Children should predict what they expect to happen and relate this to their own understanding understanding of science. They should provide a clear statement of what happened in the test. They should explain how their understanding of the science has been confirmed or changed as a result.

Example of a child's response

> I am trying to find out...
> on which surface the ball bounces best.

Before testing

> I predict that this will happen:
> The solid rubber ball will bounce best on the hard tiled floor.

> I think it will happen because:
> The tiled floor won't change shape so most of the 'bounce' will stay in the ball. When the ball lands on the carpet it flattens it a bit so some of the 'bounce' is lost.

After testing

> This is what happened:
> The ball bounced well on the tiled floor but it bounced best on the mini-trampoline. It didn't bounce at all in the sand tray and the crash mat.

> What I think now:
> The trampoline is very springy. It is made of elastic material. The solid ball is quite heavy so I think that it was the springiness in the trampoline that made the ball bounce, not the bounciness of the ball. I think a ball bearing would bounce well on the trampoline but a bouncy tennis ball wouldn't because it is not very heavy. I think that the tennis ball would bounce better on the tiled floor than a ball bearing.

Key vocabulary

Dependent on science content.

Note

In the case of the 'Example of a child's response', a further round of practical testing and reflecting on the evidence is called for in order to test out the new prediction.

What I think now

Name _____ Date _____

I am trying to find out …

Before testing

I predict that this will happen:

I think it will happen because:

After testing

This is what happened:

What I think now:

My results

National Curriculum focus
Sc1/2h use a wide range of methods, including diagrams, drawings, tables, bar charts, line graphs and ICT, to commuinicate data in an appropriate and systematic manner.

Assessment objective
The children should demonstrate that they are able to record data from a practical investigation in a systematic way.

Potential assessment activities	Assessment outcomes
Children should be told how to record their results, eg in a table. Children should have the opportunity to record data in a variety scientific topic areas.	Children should record numerical data, suggest ways in which it might be presented and offer simple explanations for their findings.
Children structure and record their results whilst carrying out a practical investigation.	Children should record numerical data in an appropriate format for presentation and draw relevant conclusions.
Children should record a series of observations over time, or record repeat measurements.	Children should able to identify and present data using an appropriate type of graph or table.

Example of a child's response

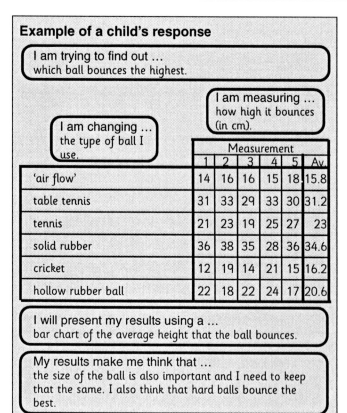

I am trying to find out ...
which ball bounces the highest.

I am changing ...
the type of ball I use.

I am measuring ...
how high it bounces (in cm).

	Measurement					
	1	2	3	4	5	Av.
'air flow'	14	16	16	15	18	15.8
table tennis	31	33	29	33	30	31.2
tennis	21	23	19	25	27	23
solid rubber	36	38	35	28	36	34.6
cricket	12	19	14	21	15	16.2
hollow rubber ball	22	18	22	24	17	20.6

I will present my results using a ...
bar chart of the average height that the ball bounces.

My results make me think that ...
the size of the ball is also important and I need to keep that the same. I also think that hard balls bounce the best.

Key vocabulary
Dependent on science content.

Note
This sheet shows just one way of recording results. Other ways include:
*   tally chart (when carrying out surveys)
*   photographs
*   drawings
*   data logging

Ways of presenting results include:
*   bar charts – for surveys, and when the variable you change is in words (like the example)
*   pie charts – for surveys
*   line graphs – when both the independent and dependent variables are numerical.

My results

Name_____ Date_____

I am trying to find out …

I am measuring …

I am changing …

	Measurement					
	1	2	3	4	5	Average

I will present my results using a …

My results make me think that …

Applying and understanding findings

National Curriculum focus

Sc1/1a that science is about thinking creatively to try to explain how living and non-living things work, and to establish links between causes and effects;

Sc1/2j use observations, measurements or other data to draw conclusions;

Sc1/2l use their scientific knowledge and understanding to explain observations, measurements or other data or conclusions.

Sc1/2m review their work and the work of others and describe its significance and limitations.

Assessment objective

The children should demonstrate that they are able to apply the findings of their investigations to explain scientific phenomena.

Potential assessment activities	Assessment Outcomes
When children have finished an investigation/ survey, they should describe what they found out, and explain why their findings are important. It is and important that the children are able to evaluate what happened and compare it to what they were expecting.	Children should be able to explain what they found out and to relate the outcome of the activity to their own scientific understanding.
When children have finished an investigation/ survey, they should compare what they found out with an established scientific theory.	Children should begin to relate their results with established scientific theory.

Example of a child's response

My investigation was about …
finding out which surface a tennis ball would bounce highest on.

I predicted that …
it would bounce highest on a hard surface and least high on a soft one.

I found out that …
it did bounce highest on a hard surface, but that the surface also has to be smooth. The ball bounced higher on the smooth concrete path than the playground or the concrete path, because they are rough. It did not bounce much at all on the crash mat which is used to give you a soft landing if you fall. The wooden hall floor is a bit springy so it lost a bit of its bounce there.

This helps to explain why …
tennis is played on a fairly hard surface. If it was played on a very hard surface the ball would probably bounce too high and the players wouldn't be able to reach it. On a very soft surface it wouldn't bounce enough. Too much grass makes the ground soft. I think that's why they cut the grass so short at Wimbledon.

Key vocabulary

Dependent upon science content.

Applying and understanding findings

Name _____ Date _____

My investigation was about …

I predicted that …

I found out that …

This helps to explain why …

Making sense of what I found out

National Curriculum focus

Sc1/1a that science is about thinking creatively to try to explain how living and non-living things work, and to establish links between causes and effects;

Sc2/2j use observations, measurements or other data to draw conclusions;

Sc2/2k decide whether these conclusions agree with any prediction made and/or whether they enable further predictions to be made;

Sc2/2l use their scientific knowledge and understanding to explain observations, measurements or other data or conclusions;

Sc2/2m review their work and the work of others and describe its significance and limitations.

Assessment objective

The children should demonstrate their ability to link their findings from practical scientific activities to their understanding of scientific processes or phenomena.

Potential assessment activity
After children have carried out an investigation, they should write about what they found out and explain the significance of their findings.

Assessment outcome
Children should identify clearly the scientific focus of their investigation. They should provide a clear statement of what happened and what they found out from their activity. They should, where appropriate, use the findings of the activity to help to explain the science behind similar scientific phenomena.

Example of a child's response

My investigation was about...
finding out which surface the ball bounced best on.

I found out that...
the solid rubber ball bounced well on the tiled floor but it bounced best on the mini-trampoline. It didn't bounce at all in the sand tray and the crash mat. The length of the wool on the carpet had a big effect on how well it bounced on different carpets.

This helps to explain why...
we use different types of balls to play different types of sports and why different sports are played on different surfaces. We play football on grass because the grass stops the ball bouncing too high. When we play football on the playground or on hard earth the ball always bounces too high. When the grass is too long it doesn't bounce enough. The grass has to be very short if you want to play cricket or tennis otherwise the ball doesn't bounce at all.

To follow this up I would like to ...
test different sports surfaces to see what is the best surface for different types of ball games. I want to see if a running track would make a good football or tennis or cricket pitch.

Key vocabulary
Dependent upon science content.

Note
In the case of the 'Example of a child's response', in a further round of practical testing, the child would need to be encouraged to focus more on ensuring a fair test so that any comparisons made would be valid.

Making sense of what I found out

Name _____ Date _____

My investigation was about …

I found out that …

This helps to explain why …

To follow this up I would like to …

Living things

National Curriculum focus

Sc2/1a that the life processes common to humans and other animals include nutrition, movement, growth and reproduction;

Sc2/1b that the life processes common to plants include growth, nutrition and reproduction.

Assessment objective

The children should demonstrate that they can identify living things, noting the similarities and differences between animals and plants.

Potential assessment activities	Assessment outcomes
Children describe the similarities and differences between living and non-living things given a stimulus – eg asked to compare a baby and a doll.	Children should be able to identify appropriate distinguishing factors such as growth, the need for sustenance, independent action.
Through discussion (group or class), children describe and collate the characteristics of living things.	Children should use appropriate vocabulary to describe the characteristics including growth, feeding, breathing, reproduction, movement.
Working in groups, children begin to define the differences between animals and plants.	Children should produce two lists based upon the similarities and differences they perceive between animals and plants.
On the PCM children record, using a combination of drawings and text, their understanding of the characteristics of living things and the criteria which distinguishes animals from plants.	Children should identify appropriate similarities and differences using the correct terminology where possible.

Example of a child's response

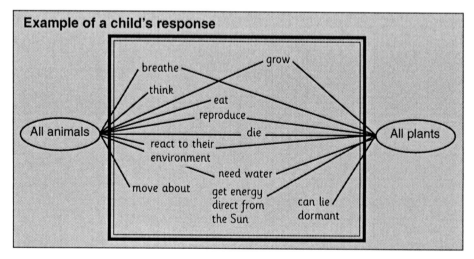

Key vocabulary
Breathe
Grow
Reproduce

Notes

Plants breathe in and out the same gases as animals. Green plants also photosynthesize (they use the energy from the Sun to extract carbon from carbon dioxide). Children are keen to say that animals think – meaning that they have a greater intelligence than plants (think isn't really the best word for it!). As seeds, plants can lie dormant, within limits, until the appropriate conditions for germination occur. Most children feel that 'eat' isn't the appropriate word for what plants do.

Living things

All living things do certain things – that is how we know that they are alive. Some things only plants do, other only animals. Think what those 'life processes' could be and write them in the box.

All plants

Draw lines to link these life processes to animals, plants or both.

All animals

Sorting key

National Curriculum focus
Sc2/4a to make and use keys;
Sc2/4b how locally occurring animals and plants can be identified and assigned to groups.

Assessment objective
The children should demonstrate that they can identify observable features in order to be able to sort and categorize groups of animals or plants.

Potential assessment activities	Assessment outcomes
Children identify observable similarities and differences between a group of animals and plants. (You will need to have six flowering plants, tree leaves or mini-beasts available for observation.)	Children should be able to identify observable features which distinguish one specimen from another.
Play 'yes/no' games such as 'Guess Who..?' to help children to identify and frame categoric questions appropriately.	Children should use appropriate vocabulary to form the questions in order to separate the groups and specimens.
Children use ready-made sorting keys to identify specimens that they have found or have been provided with. (*The Observer's Book of Pond Life* has a good example of a sorting key.)	Working in a practical situation children should make observations appropriate to the questions being asked by the key.
On the PCM children identify categoric questions which can be used to sort and name specimens which are available to the children.	Children should use appropriate scientific criteria when identifying the features by which the specimens will be sorted.

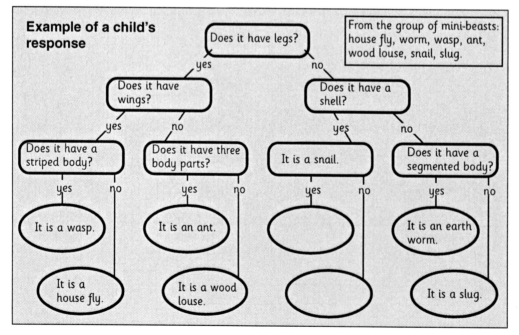

Example of a child's response

From the group of mini-beasts: house fly, worm, wasp, ant, wood louse, snail, slug.

Key vocabulary
Will be very dependent upon the specimens that are being sorted.

Sorting key

Name

Date

Use this sheet to sort a collection of plants or animals found in your locality according to observable features.

question

item

I am trying to sort …

yes   no

yes   no   yes   no

yes   no   yes   no   yes   no   yes   no

Assessing Science

31

Food chains

National Curriculum focus
Sc2/5d to use food chains to show feeding relationships in a habitat;
Sc2/5e about how nearly all food chains start with a green plant.

Assessment objective
The children should demonstrate that they can identify the feeding relationships between animals and plants within an ecosystem.

Potential assessment activities	Assessment outcomes
Children identify the relationship between a set of common animals and plants in terms of '… is eaten by …'.	Children should know the feeding habits of a small range of common animals.
Children carry out research to discover the feeding requirements of a range of animals.	Children should collate this data in an appropriate format such as on data cards or in a computer database.
Children discuss, as a class or group, the flow of energy, in the form of food, from the Sun to higher or tertiary predators.	Children should understand the importance of the Sun and plants to all food chains.
On the PCM children identify the feeding relationships within a small system.	Children should use appropriate plants and animals when producing their chain.

Key vocabulary
Carnivore
Ecosystem
Herbivore
Omnivore
Predator
Prey
Primary producer

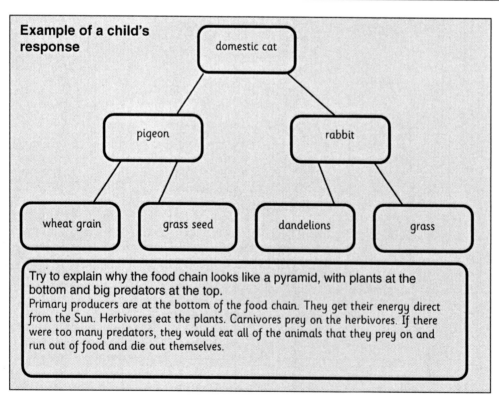

Example of a child's response

Try to explain why the food chain looks like a pyramid, with plants at the bottom and big predators at the top.
Primary producers are at the bottom of the food chain. They get their energy direct from the Sun. Herbivores eat the plants. Carnivores prey on the herbivores. If there were too many predators, they would eat all of the animals that they prey on and run out of food and die out themselves.

Food chains

Name _____ Date _____

Identify the plants and animals that make up this chain.

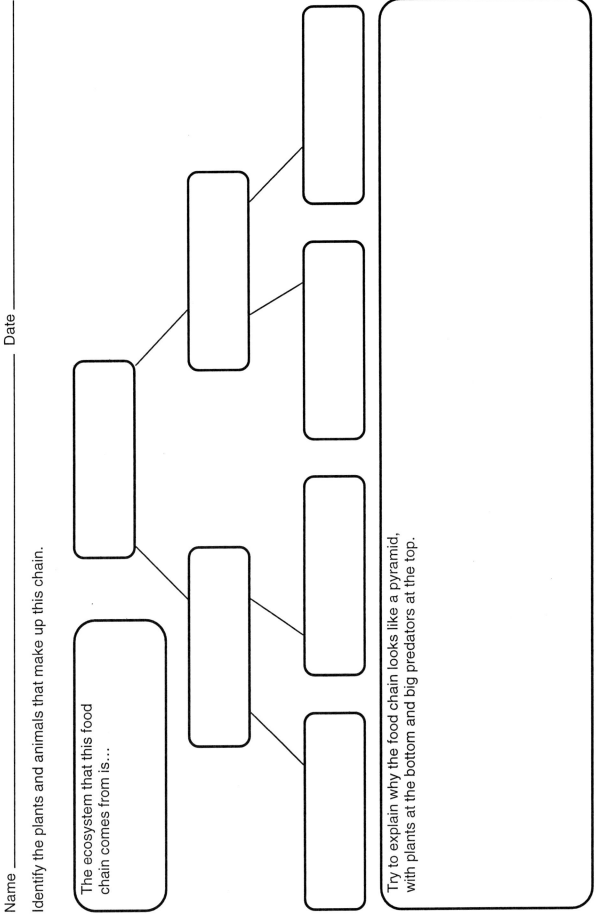

The ecosystem that this food chain comes from is...

Try to explain why the food chain looks like a pyramid, with plants at the bottom and big predators at the top.

Blood circulation

National Curriculum focus

Sc2/2c   that the heart acts as a pump to circulate the blood through vessels around the body, including through the lungs;

Sc2/2d   about the effect of exercise and rest on pulse rate.

Assessment objective

The children should demonstrate their understanding of the human blood circulatory system.

Potential assessment activities	Assessment outcomes
The children identify the key features of blood circulation.	Children should know the purpose of blood circulating within the body (supplying muscles with food and oxygen and removing waste).
Children find their pulses and record their pulse rates before and after exercise and discuss why they change.	Children should identify the need for extra oxygen and food to be delivered to the muscles.
Children discuss, as a class or group, the need for a 'transport system' between organs within the body.	Children should describe the role of the heart (pump), lungs (air exchange), small intestine (filter for nutrients) and kidneys (waste filter).
On the PCM children identify the key terminology and annotate drawings to describe the circulation of blood within the human body. (The list of key vocabulary on the PCM may be deleted for reasons of differentiation.)	Children should use appropriate vocabulary in a scientifically correct way to explain the role that blood, and the major circulation organs that it interacts with, perform.

Example of a child's response

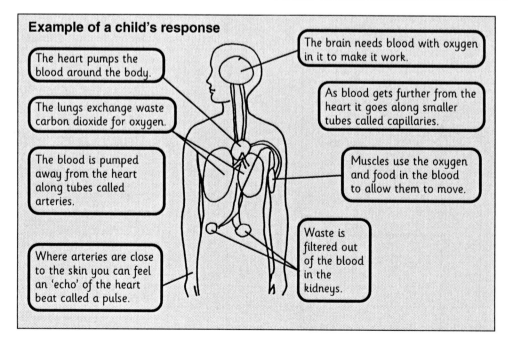

The heart pumps the blood around the body.

The lungs exchange waste carbon dioxide for oxygen.

The blood is pumped away from the heart along tubes called arteries.

Where arteries are close to the skin you can feel an 'echo' of the heart beat called a pulse.

The brain needs blood with oxygen in it to make it work.

As blood gets further from the heart it goes along smaller tubes called capillaries.

Muscles use the oxygen and food in the blood to allow them to move.

Waste is filtered out of the blood in the kidneys.

Key vocabulary

Arteries
Blood
Brain
Capillaries
Carbon dioxide
Heart
Kidneys
Lungs
Muscles
Oxygen
Veins

Blood circulation

Name

Date

Add to this drawing to explain what you think happens as blood circulates in our bodies. Write notes in the boxes to explain your drawing.

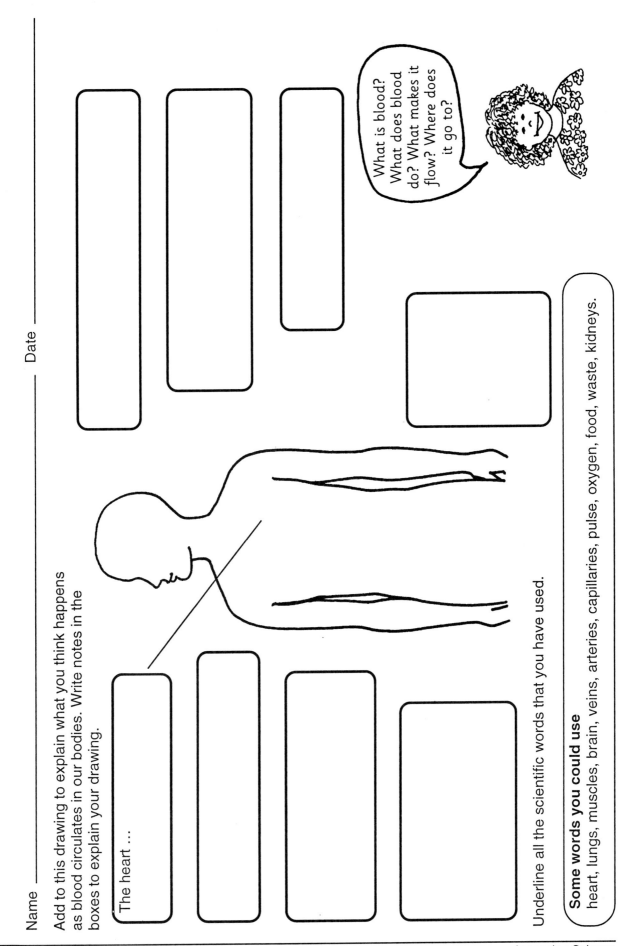

What is blood? What does blood do? What makes it flow? Where does it go to?

The heart ...

Underline all the scientific words that you have used.

Some words you could use
heart, lungs, muscles, brain, veins, arteries, capillaries, pulse, oxygen, food, waste, kidneys.

Bones and muscles

National Curriculum focus
Sc2/2e that humans and some other animals have skeletons and muscles to support and protect their bodies and to help them to move.

Assessment objective
The children should demonstrate their understanding of how muscles and bones work together in humans to provide structure and movement.

Potential assessment activities	Assessment outcomes
Children explore their own bodies to identify bones and muscles.	Children should be able to point out muscles and bones within their body.
Children draw a representation of their skeleton, identifying joints as gaps between bones. (This can be done on the PCM.)	Children should place joints in appropriate places, particularly on limbs.
Children discuss, as a class or group, how their bodies move and explain the part muscles play in this.	Children should describe the changes in muscles as they contract and relax and relate this to body movements (particularly limbs).
On the PCM children identify the key terminology and annotate drawings to describe the skeletal and musculature structure of the human body.	Children should use appropriate vocabulary in a scientifically correct way to demonstrate their understanding of how muscles and bones interact to achieve movement.

Example of a child's response

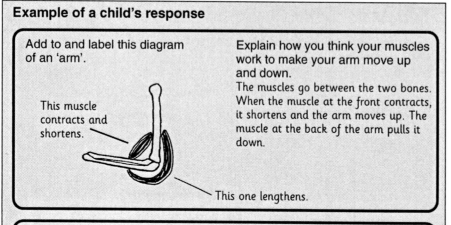

Add to and label this diagram of an 'arm'.

This muscle contracts and shortens.

This one lengthens.

Explain how you think your muscles work to make your arm move up and down.
The muscles go between the two bones. When the muscle at the front contracts, it shortens and the arm moves up. The muscle at the back of the arm pulls it down.

Our muscles and bones are joined together because ...
bones give our bodies shape. To make our bodies change shape and to make them move, our bones must move. Muscles pull on our bones to make them change position so that our bodies can move.

Key vocabulary
Antagonistic Pair
Bone
Joint
Muscles
Skeleton

Note
Most muscles work in pairs – one to move the body part, the other to move it back (antagonistic pairs). Joints act as pivot points. The muscles make the bones move about the pivot point. The muscles in the upper arm which work around the elbow are the most accessible for examination.

Bones and muscles

Our skeleton looks like this …

What do all of the bones and muscles inside us do?
Draw and explain how you think it all works.

Explain how you think your muscles work to make your arm move up and down.

Add to and label this diagram of an 'arm'.

Our muscles and bones are joined together because …

Underline all the important scientific words that you have used.

Digestive system

National Curriculum focus
Sc2/1a that the life processes common to humans and other animals include nutrition, movement, growth
and reproduction.

Assessment objective
The children should demonstrate their understanding of what happens as food is digested.

Potential assessment activities	Assessment outcomes
Children identify the four key parts of the digestive process and the names of the organs involved through whole class discussion.	Children should know the parts involved in the digestive process (mouth, stomach, small and large intestines).
Children write a story telling of the journey of a piece of food.	The story should demonstrate an awareness of the full digestive process, being scientifically accurate.
Children discuss, as a class or group, the overall process and the individual parts played by the mouth, stomach, small and large intestines.	Children should describe the roles of the various body parts in the digestive process and be aware of how these parts work together.
On the PCM children identify the key terminology and annotate the drawing to describe the process of digestion within the human body. (The list of key vocabulary on the PCM may be deleted for reasons of differentiation.)	Children should use appropriate vocabulary in a scientifically correct way to describe and explain the different sections of the digestive process.

Example of a child's response

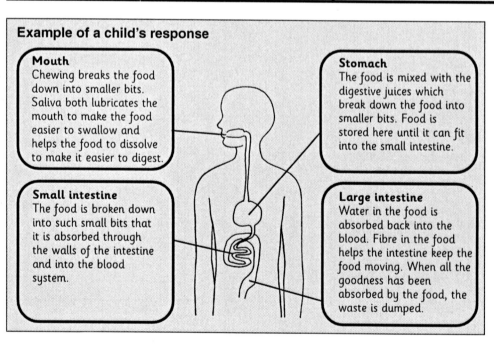

Mouth
Chewing breaks the food down into smaller bits. Saliva both lubricates the mouth to make the food easier to swallow and helps the food to dissolve to make it easier to digest.

Stomach
The food is mixed with the digestive juices which break down the food into smaller bits. Food is stored here until it can fit into the small intestine.

Small intestine
The food is broken down into such small bits that it is absorbed through the walls of the intestine and into the blood system.

Large intestine
Water in the food is absorbed back into the blood. Fibre in the food helps the intestine keep the food moving. When all the goodness has been absorbed by the food, the waste is dumped.

Key vocabulary
Digestion
Fibre
Intestine
Saliva
Stomach
Teeth

Digestive system

Name _____ Date _____

Draw and explain what you think happens as food is eaten and makes its way through the body. Try to use the correct scientific words where you can. Clearly identify the parts of the body you are describing.

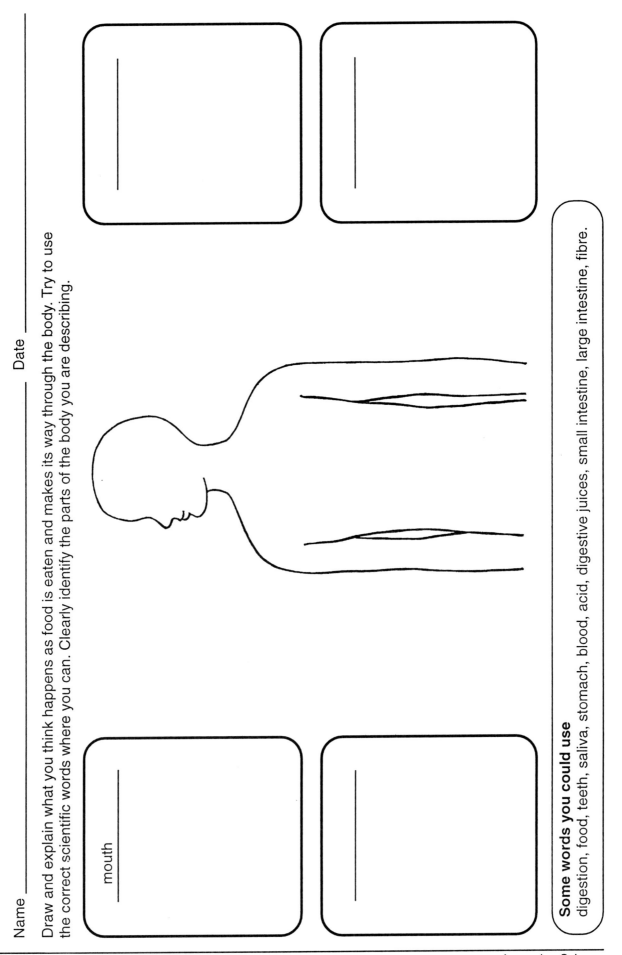

mouth _____

Some words you could use
digestion, food, teeth, saliva, stomach, blood, acid, digestive juices, small intestine, large intestine, fibre.

Eat well!

National Curriculum focus

Sc2/2b that food is needed for activity and for growth, and that an adequate and varied diet is needed to keep healthy.

Assessment objective

The children should demonstrate their understanding of healthy eating styles.

Potential assessment activities	Assessment outcomes
Children identify and sort foods into three categories: GO (energy foods), GROW (proteins), and GLOW (health promoting foods).	Children should demonstrate a knowledge of the importance of food and an awareness of the basic food groups.
Children discuss, as a class or group, the merits and uses of different food groups.	Children should demonstrate an awareness of why we need to eat a balance of foods from different groups to promote and maintain health.
Children produce a poster exemplifying the different food groups (drawn or using pictures from magazines). Children discuss the effects of having too much or too little of each of the food groups.	Children should describe the effects of having too little or too much of foods from particular groups and that excess intake is stored as fat. They should be able to sort foods into the appropriate categories.
On the PCM children identify the key terminology and provide examples of the different food groups. (The list of key vocabulary on the PCM may be deleted for reasons of differentiation.)	Children should use appropriate vocabulary in a scientifically correct way to explain the differences between, and the importance of, each of the food groups.

Example of a child's response

Protein
Foods which are full of protein help our bodies to grow and mend themselves if they are ill or have been injured.

Carbohydrates
These foods provide energy to help us be active. They can either be sugars which provide energy quickly, or starches which provide energy over a longer period of time.

Fats
Foods which are fatty provide a lot of energy. Any energy foods that we eat but don't use straight away are stored as fat in our bodies.

Vitamins
Foods which have substances which help to keep you healthy.

Minerals
Foods to help the body grow properly.

Fibre
Foods which help the digestion system to work properly.

Key vocabulary
Carbohydrates
Fats
Fibre
Minerals
Protein
Vitamins

Eat well!

Name _____ Date _____

There are three main food groups. We need a balance of these, together with fibre, minerals and vitamins to keep healthy.

Try to explain why we need these different types of food and give some examples of each.

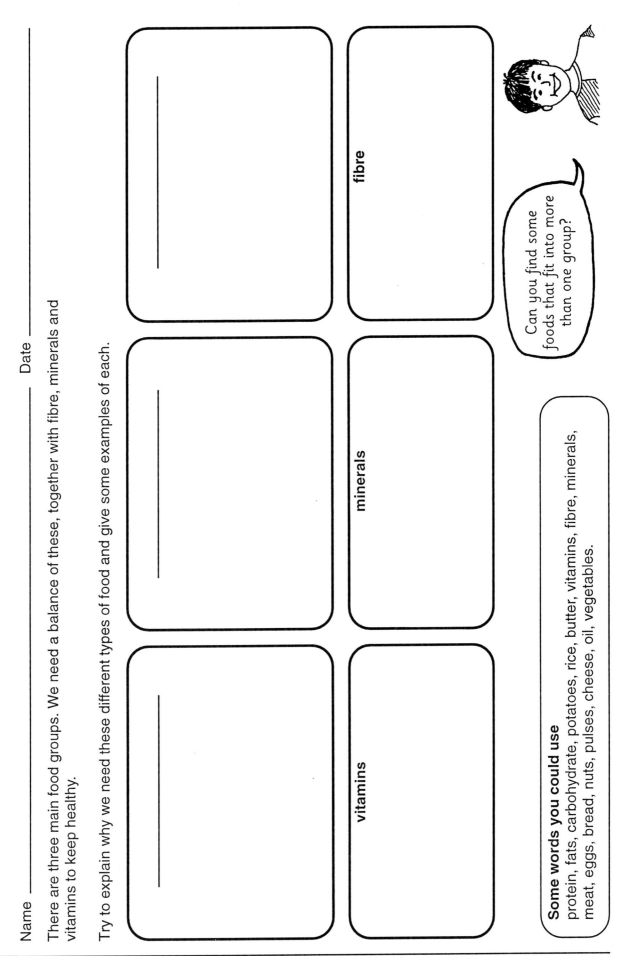

vitamins

minerals

fibre

Can you find some foods that fit into more than one group?

Some words you could use
protein, fats, carbohydrate, potatoes, rice, butter, vitamins, fibre, minerals, meat, eggs, bread, nuts, pulses, cheese, oil, vegetables.

Keeping healthy

National Curriculum focus

Sc2/2b about the need for food for activity and growth, and about the importance of an adequate and varied diet for health;

Sc2/2d about the effect of exercise and rest on the pulse rate;

Sc2/2g about the effects on the human body of tobacco, alcohol and other drugs, and how these relate to their personal health.

Assessment objective

The children should demonstrate their understanding of factors which are detrimental to a healthy life style.

Potential assessment activities	Assessment outcomes
Through a brainstorm, children identify the factors consistent with healthy and non-healthy life styles. Children discuss, as a class or group, how these factors affect health.	Children should demonstrate an awareness of the importance of diet, exercise, rest and the avoidance of harmful drugs.
Children produce a poster exemplifying a healthy life-style and warning against the effects of a non-healthy one. Children discuss the balance of these factors in terms of an appropriate amount and type of each (food, rest, exercise, TLC, use of drugs).	Children should describe the effects of having too little or too much of each of those factors and why some should be avoided completely.
On the PCM children identify the factors to avoid and provide examples of each different group.	Children should use appropriate vocabulary in a scientifically correct way to identify the factors which will lead to a healthy life style.

Key vocabulary
Diet
Drugs
Exercise
Nutrition
Rest

Example of a child's response

Tobacco
Tobacco can kill you. If you smoke, it clogs up your lungs so that you can't breathe properly, so your body can't get all the oxygen it needs.

Rest
If you don't get enough rest, your body doesn't have time to recover and gets tired.

Alcohol
This damages your liver so that it can't make and store special food for your body properly. Alcohol makes you unable to think clearly or fast enough to do things like drive safely.

Food
If you don't eat enough or a good balance of food, your body doesn't grow properly and you don't have enough energy. If you eat too much or the wrong type of foods, then you get fat.

Exercise
If you don't get enough regular exercise, your muscles don't grow strong enough. If you do too much exercise you can damage your body as well.

Keeping healthy

Identify some of the things that can have a harmful effect on our bodies.
Try to explain what the problems are.

tobacco

alcohol

Healthy heart

National Curriculum focus
Sc2/2c   that the heart acts as a pump to circulate the blood through vessels around the body, including through the lungs;
Sc2/2d   about the effect of exercise and rest on pulse rate.

Assessment objective
The children should demonstrate their understanding of the workings of the heart.

Potential assessment activities	Assessment outcomes
Children discuss, as a class or group, what the heart does and how it changes in response to physical stimulus (exercise).	Children should know that the heart pumps blood round the body. As the body needs more or less energy delivering to the muscles, the heart will speed up or slow down.
Children, in groups, design and present a piece of drama or a poster to show how a heart pumps blood.	Children should model the action of the heart accurately.
Children find their pulses and record their pulse rates before and after exercise and discuss why it changes.	Children should be able to find their pulse and measure it accurately. They should understand that their pulse increases because their heart is pumping faster.
On the PCM children label the diagram and write explanations to show their understanding of how the heart works.	Children should use appropriate vocabulary in a scientifically correct way to identify the key parts of the heart. Children working at a higher level should be able to identify that the heart is made of two pumps which work together – one half pumps blood from the body to the lungs and the other from the lungs to the rest of the body.

Key vocabulary
Heart
Lungs
Muscles
Valve

Example of a child's response

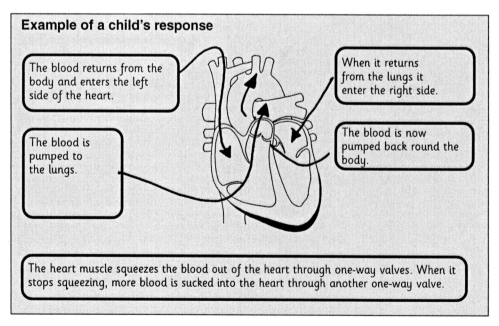

The blood returns from the body and enters the left side of the heart.

The blood is pumped to the lungs.

When it returns from the lungs it enter the right side.

The blood is now pumped back round the body.

The heart muscle squeezes the blood out of the heart through one-way valves. When it stops squeezing, more blood is sucked into the heart through another one-way valve.

Healthy heart

Name _____ Date _____

Look at the drawing of a human heart. In the boxes explain what it does and how you think it works. Use the correct scientific words where you can.

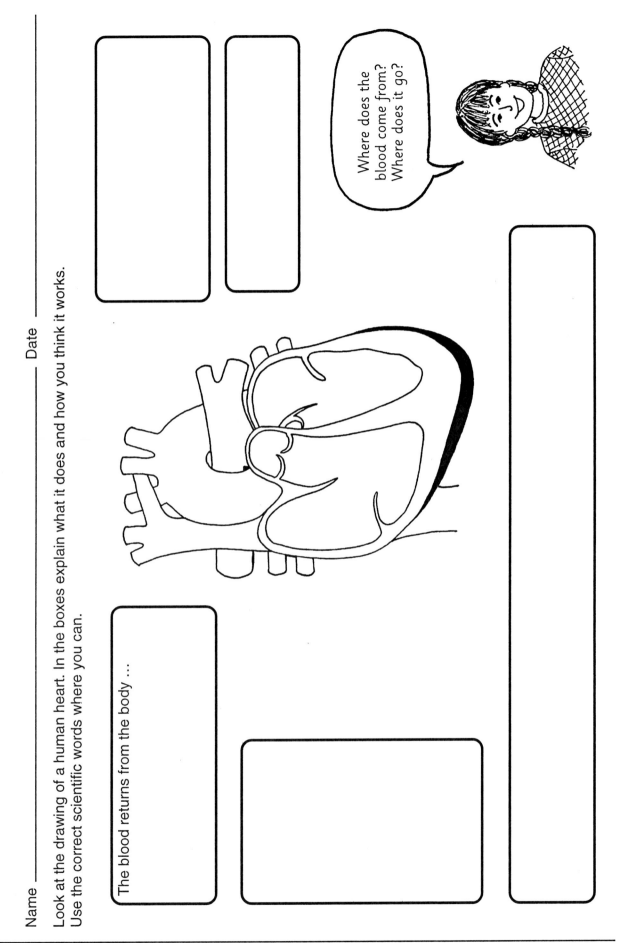

Where does the blood come from? Where does it go?

The blood returns from the body ....

Teething trouble

National Curriculum focus
Sc2/2a about the functions and care of teeth.

Assessment objective
The children should demonstrate their understanding of the function and care of teeth.

Potential assessment activities	Assessment outcomes
Children use the packaging from teeth cleaning products to identify the importance of dental care and the causes of dental problems. They should relate what they have found out to their own experience.	Children should identify tooth decay, gum disease, bad breath as being problems and the non-removal of food debris as being a major cause. Children should describe how they clean their teeth and relate this to how dental problems can be avoided or reduced.
Working in groups, children look at different types of real teeth, eg a sheep's tooth and a canine tooth, and identify what they are used for.	Children should identify the different functions of different types of teeth (eg canine teeth are used for cutting food, sheep's teeth for grinding).
Working in groups, children research the internal structure of teeth (they can record their findings on the PCM).	Children should draw accurately and describe the internal structure of the tooth, making use of appropriate terminology.
On the PCM children identify and describe the function of different types of teeth and explain the need for careful dental hygiene.	Children should use appropriate vocabulary in a scientifically correct way to identify and describe types of teeth, the structure of a tooth and also the causes of dental problems.

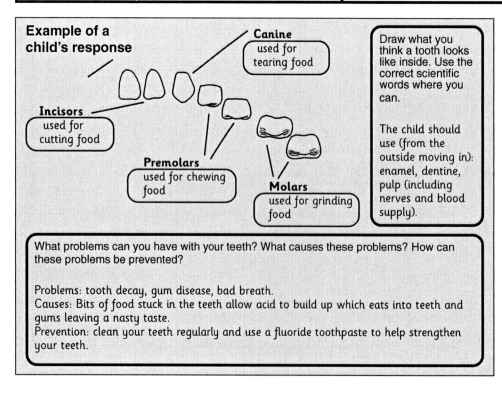

Example of a child's response

Incisors
used for cutting food

Canine
used for tearing food

Premolars
used for chewing food

Molars
used for grinding food

Draw what you think a tooth looks like inside. Use the correct scientific words where you can.

The child should use (from the outside moving in): enamel, dentine, pulp (including nerves and blood supply).

What problems can you have with your teeth? What causes these problems? How can these problems be prevented?

Problems: tooth decay, gum disease, bad breath.
Causes: Bits of food stuck in the teeth allow acid to build up which eats into teeth and gums leaving a nasty taste.
Prevention: clean your teeth regularly and use a fluoride toothpaste to help strengthen your teeth.

Key vocabulary
Canine
Dentine
Enamel
Gums
Incisors
Molars
Premolars
Pulp
Teeth

Teething trouble

Name _____ Date _____

You have different kinds of teeth in your mouth.
What are they called? Why do they look different?
Try to explain what different jobs they do.

Draw what you think a tooth looks like inside. Use the correct scientific words where you can.

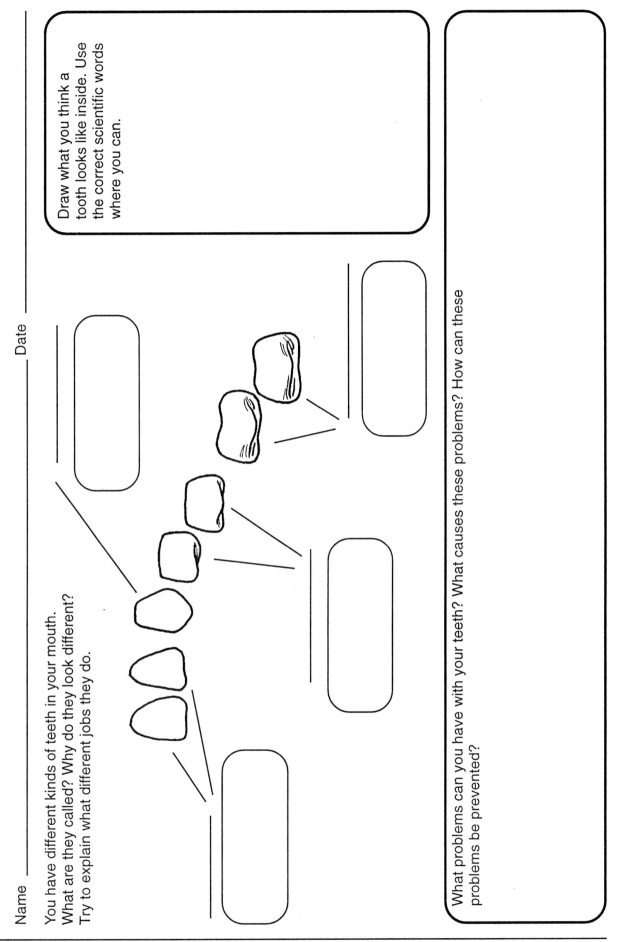

What problems can you have with your teeth? What causes these problems? How can these problems be prevented?

Plant parts

National Curriculum focus
Sc2/3c that the root anchors the plant, and that water and minerals are taken in through the root and transported through the stem to other parts of the plant.

Assessment objective
The children should demonstrate their ability to identify the various parts of a flowering plant and describe what they do.

Potential assessment activities	Assessment outcomes
Children play naming and matching games to identify the various external parts of green plants.	Children should know leaf, flower, stem and root.
Children, in groups, discuss what they think different parts of the plant might do.	Children should describe the function of the leaf, flower, stem and root, noting that the leaf is where the plant makes its food.
Working in groups, the children are given a flower in order to identify and describe the different parts of the flower head (daffodils and tulips are quite good for this). They could record their findings on the PCM, if the picture is covered over before the sheet is copied.	Children should identify and name the parts of the flower head (petal, stigma, stamen, anther, stamen).
Children compare different flower heads and explain what each of the different parts do.	Children should explain what the parts of the flower head do.
On the PCM, children identify and describe the function of different parts of a plant.	Children should use appropriate vocabulary in a scientifically correct way to identify and describe the role of the plant parts.

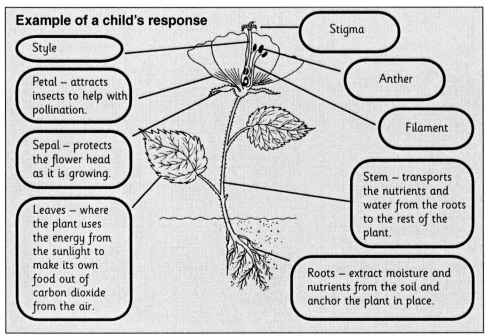

Example of a child's response

Style

Petal – attracts insects to help with pollination.

Sepal – protects the flower head as it is growing.

Leaves – where the plant uses the energy from the sunlight to make its own food out of carbon dioxide from the air.

Stigma

Anther

Filament

Stem – transports the nutrients and water from the roots to the rest of the plant.

Roots – extract moisture and nutrients from the soil and anchor the plant in place.

Key vocabulary
Anther
Filament
Flower
Leaf
Nutrients
Petal
Roots
Sepal
Stamen
Stem
Stigma
Style

Plant parts

Name _____ Date _____

All flowering plants have certain parts in common – but what are they called and what do they do? Name and explain these plant parts.

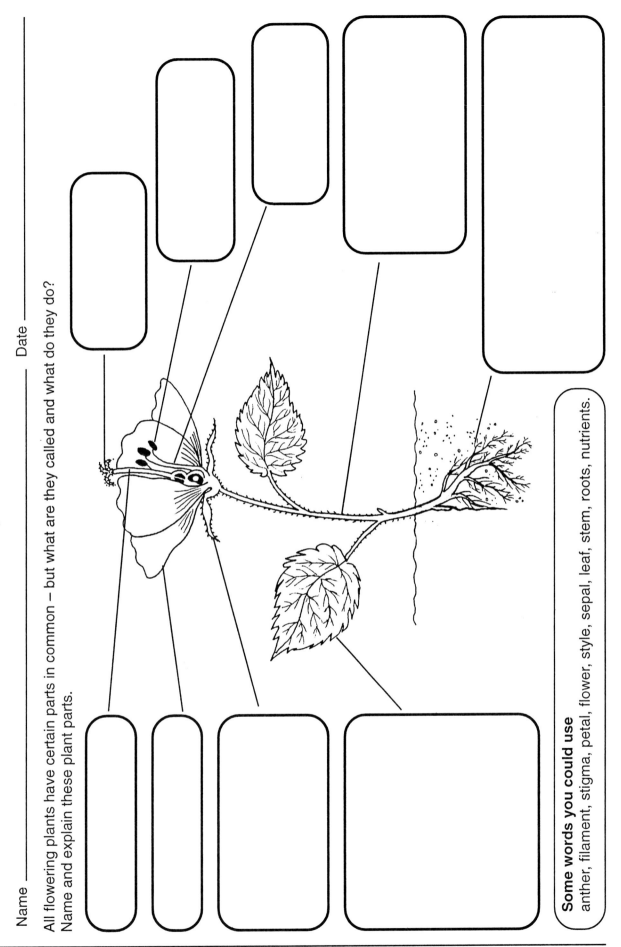

Some words you could use
anther, filament, stigma, petal, flower, style, sepal, leaf, stem, roots, nutrients.

Healthy plants

National Curriculum focus
Sc2/3a the effect of light, air, water and temperature on plant growth;
Sc2/3b the role of the leaf in producing new material for growth.

Assessment objective
The children should demonstrate their understanding of the conditions required for healthy plant growth.

Potential assessment activities	Assessment outcomes
Through a brainstorm, children identify and describe the factors that might affect the quality of plant growth (light, warmth, water, growing medium, nutrients, air).	Children should demonstrate that they know the factors which affect plant growth.
Children discuss, as a class or group, how these factors might affect the growth of plants.	Children should be able to identify and describe the affects, on a plant, of the removal of one or more of these necessary conditions (eg, no light – yellowing leaves).
Children design and carry out an investigation to study the effects on plant growth of one of these factors (amount of water, duration of light,...).	Children should demonstrate that they are able to plan an investigation based upon the identification of key variables of plant growth.
Children discuss how the growing conditions for some plants vary from those required for another (eg cactus and water lily).	Children should relate the varying needs of plants to the differences between habitats.
On the PCM children identify what plants need and through writing and drawing explain how they affect growth.	Children should use appropriate vocabulary in a scientifically correct way to identify the factors which influence the growth of plants.

Example of a child's response

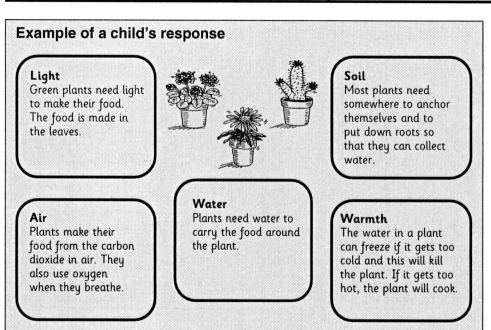

Light
Green plants need light to make their food. The food is made in the leaves.

Soil
Most plants need somewhere to anchor themselves and to put down roots so that they can collect water.

Air
Plants make their food from the carbon dioxide in air. They also use oxygen when they breathe.

Water
Plants need water to carry the food around the plant.

Warmth
The water in a plant can freeze if it gets too cold and this will kill the plant. If it gets too hot, the plant will cook.

Key vocabulary
Carbon dioxide
Freeze
Habitat
Oxygen
Photosynthesis
Roots

Healthy plants

Name _____ Date _____

Identify the things that plants need for them to be healthy. Try to explain why these things are so important. Use the correct scientific words where you can.

Plant cycles

National Curriculum focus
Sc2/3d   about the parts of the flower and their role in the life cycle of flowering plants, including pollination, seed formation, seed dispersal and germination.

Assessment objective
The children should demonstrate their understanding of the life cycle of a flowering plant.

Potential assessment activities	Assessment outcomes
Children place pictures on the PCM (of a plant at different stages of its life cycle) in the correct order.	Children should know the order of a plant life cycle.
Children, in groups, discuss what they think is happening in each of the pictures on the PCM.	Children should describe the main feature of each part of the life cycle (germination, flower production, seed production, seed dispersal,...).
Working in groups, children grow plants from seeds and record the different stages of the cycle (using written descriptions, drawings or photos).	Children should be able to make accurate records and compare their observations with an 'expected' cycle.
Children compare different flowering plants and describe the similarities and differences in their cycles.	Children note differences such as the time required to grow, dispersal methods, types of flower, etc.
Children identify and describe the function of different parts of a flowering plant's life cycle.	Children should use appropriate vocabulary in a scientifically correct way to identify and describe the life cycle of a flowering plant (see 'Example of a child's response', below).

Example of a child's response

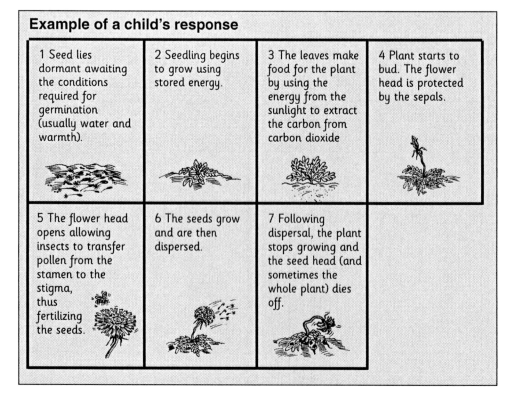

1 Seed lies dormant awaiting the conditions required for germination (usually water and warmth).	2 Seedling begins to grow using stored energy.	3 The leaves make food for the plant by using the energy from the sunlight to extract the carbon from carbon dioxide	4 Plant starts to bud. The flower head is protected by the sepals.
5 The flower head opens allowing insects to transfer pollen from the stamen to the stigma, thus fertilizing the seeds.	6 The seeds grow and are then dispersed.	7 Following dispersal, the plant stops growing and the seed head (and sometimes the whole plant) dies off.	

Key vocabulary
Cycle
Dispersal
Flower
Germination
Leaf
Pollen
Pollination
Roots
Sepal
Stamen
Stigma

Plant cycles

Cut out these pictures and stick them on another piece of paper in the correct order.

Use appropriate scientific words where you can to explain what is happening in each box.

Some words you could use
leaf, roots, light, warmth, pollination, germination, dispersal, stigma, stamen, water, sepal.

Where/how does it live?

National Curriculum focus
Sc2/5b   about the different plants and animals found in different habitats;
Sc2/5c   how animals and plants in two different habitats are suited to their environment.

Assessment objective
The children should demonstrate their understanding of the ways in which animals and plants are suited to their environment.

Potential assessment activities	Assessment outcomes
Through a brainstorm children identify and describe different types of habitat and the life that might be found there (eg, sea-shore, forest, desert, pond).	Children should demonstrate that they know that different animals and plants are able to thrive in different conditions or habitats.
Children discuss, as a class or group, how these habitats might influence the plants and animals living there.	Children should be able to identify why particular animals or plants are suited to particular habitats.
Children design an animal or plant that would be suited to a particular environment. Children discuss how some similar animals and plants can be found in different habitats.	Children should demonstrate that they are becoming aware of the environmental factors which affect animals and plants and make the animals and plants suited to a particular habitat.
On the PCM children make observations of a particular animal or plant and make deductions about the likely habitat that it lives in.	Children should use appropriate vocabulary in a scientifically correct way to identify the factors which influence the animal or plant to live in a particular habitat.

Key vocabulary
Camouflage
Climate
Environment
Habitat

Example of a child's response

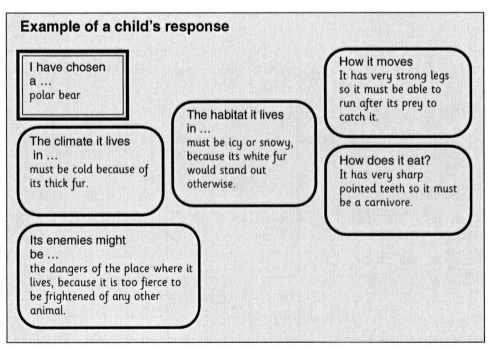

I have chosen a ...
polar bear

The climate it lives in ...
must be cold because of its thick fur.

The habitat it lives in ...
must be icy or snowy, because its white fur would stand out otherwise.

How it moves
It has very strong legs so it must be able to run after its prey to catch it.

How does it eat?
It has very sharp pointed teeth so it must be a carnivore.

Its enemies might be ...
the dangers of the place where it lives, because it is too fierce to be frightened of any other animal.

Where/how does it live?

Name _____

Date _____

Choose an animal or a plant. By observing it closely, what can you say about it?

I have chosen a ...

The habitat it lives in ...

The climate it lives in ...

You may be able to tell how a plant reproduces or disperses it seeds, or how an animal moves.

Try to show the difference between what you can **observe** and what you **know**.

Micro-organisms

National Curriculum focus
Sc2/5f   that micro-organisms are living organisms that are often too small to be seen, and that they may be beneficial or harmful.

Assessment objective
The children should demonstrate their understanding of the role played by micro-organisms.

Potential assessment activities	Assessment outcomes
Children brainstorm to identify micro-organisms (bacteria, germs, viruses, yeast,...).	Children should know some of the types of micro-organisms.
Children, in groups, discuss what they think these micro-organisms might do.	Children should identify some harmful effects (illnesses) and some beneficial effects (bread).
Children identify and describe some of the beneficial uses of micro-organisms (decomposers, raising agents, fermenting and brewing,...). Children identify and describe some of the harmful effects of micro-organisms (mainly illnesses and food spoilage).	Children should provide a range of examples by collecting newspaper/magazine articles and labels from products (eg yoghurt, wine, antiseptics), avoiding cleaning products due to the danger to the children.
On the PCM children describe the role of micro-organisms in a variety of situations.	Children should use appropriate vocabulary in a scientifically correct way to identify the effects of the micro-organisms. They should identify those which are harmful and those which are useful.

Example of a child's response

compost heap
Decomposers break down the once living stuff into nutrients which go into the soil.

bread
The yeast in the dough starts to grow. As it does it makes carbon dioxide which makes the bread rise.

sewage works
Decomposers break down the water into a form which can add to the nutrients in the soil.

yoghurt
Micro-organisms cause the milk to change and to become thicker, making yoghurt.

germs
These micro-organisms can irritate parts of the body and the body feels ill – sore throats, coughs and sneezes.

Key vocabulary
Carbon dioxide
Decomposers
Micro-organism
Nutrients

Micro-organisms

Name _____   Date _____

Explain what the micro-organisms are doing in each of these examples.

compost heap

bread

sewage works

yoghurt

germs

Show which of these you think are useful and which are harmful to us.

Properties and uses of materials

National Curriculum focus
Sc3/1a to compare everyday materials and objects on the basis of their material properties, including hardness, strength, flexibility and magnetic behaviour, and relate these properties to everyday uses of the materials;
Sc3/1b that some materials are better thermal insulators than others;
Sc3/1c that some materials are better electrical conductors than others.

Assessment objective
The children should demonstrate that they can link the properties of materials to the uses to which they are put.

Potential assessment activities	Assessment outcomes
Children identify some of the common materials used in the classroom and link them to how they are being used.	Children should be able to name common materials (glass, wood,..) and identify the property(ies) which have resulted in them being used for particular purposes.
Through discussion (group or class), children describe the properties of materials and identify materials which are similar.	Children should use appropriate vocabulary to describe the properties. These should relate to the material rather than the object.
Working in groups, children design simple tests to compare the different properties of materials (hardness, flexibility, electrical conductivity, etc). Children describe the similarities and differences between a range of different materials in terms of their properties and uses.	Working in a practical situation, children should plan simple fair tests to be able to compare (eg) hardness, elasticity, strength, etc. They should be able to make comparisons between different materials and their properties.
On the PCM children record observations (using a range of appropriate senses) and the outcome of simple tests to make a comparative study of common materials.	Children should use appropriate scientific criteria when identifying the properties by which the materials will be tested and sorted.

Example of a child's response

What makes it useful?

Materials	hard	light	strong	transparent	plastic	elastic	Uses of the materials
wood	✓	✓	✓				doors, tables
glass	✓		✓	✔			windows, drinking glasses
rubber		✓	✓		✔	✔	rubber bands, tyres
play dough		✓			✔		making models
cotton		✓	✓			✔	clothing
cling film		✓		✔	✔		wrapping food

Key vocabulary
Elastic
Electrical conductor
Hard
Magnetic
Plastic
Rigid
Strong
Thermal insulator
Translucent

Properties and uses of materials

Name _____ Date _____

Identify a range of potential properties of materials. Relate these properties to a list of different materials. How can you show the extent to which a material has a property?

Look around your class or school to identify the uses that have been made of these materials.

What makes it useful?

Uses of the materials

Materials

(strength)   (hardness)   (electrical conductor?)

(magnetic?)   (flexibility)   (heat insulator)

Comparing rocks and soils

National Curriculum focus
Sc3/1d to describe and group rocks and soils on the basis of characteristics, including appearance, texture and permeability.

Assessment objective
The children should demonstrate that they can identify the similarities and differences between different soil or rock samples.

Potential assessment activities	Assessment outcomes
Children sort or order rocks or soil according to their own criteria (page 31, *Sorting Key*, could be used).	Children should identify appropriate scientific criteria by which to sort, and use these criteria to place the samples in appropriate categories.
Through discussion (group or class), children describe the characteristics of a rock or soil sample by comparing it with another.	Children should use appropriate vocabulary to describe the characteristics of rocks or soils.
Working in groups, children design simple tests to compare different samples. Children describe the similarities and differences between a range of samples.	Working in a practical situation, children should plan simple fair tests to be able to compare rocks or soils, eg hardness, porosity. They should be able to make comparisons between the different samples.
On the PCM children record, using a combination of drawings and text, observations (using a range of appropriate senses) and the outcome of simple tests.	Children should use appropriate scientific and descriptive terminology to report on the appearance and texture of each sample. Terminology and any tests used should be consistent across samples.

Key vocabulary
Absorbent
Hard
Igneous
Metamorphic
Particles
Permeable
Sedimentary

Example of a child's response

Rock or soil sample	Appearance	Texture	My test results
garden soil	dark, strong	crumbles a bit, sticky when wet	gets muddy when mixed with water
sandy soil	light coloured, lots of grains	gritty, rough sharp	water runs through it
peaty soil	very dark	a bit like cotton wool	soaks up water like a sponge

Notes
Rocks can be rubbed together to determine the order of hardness; the harder one will mark the softer one. Children could be encouraged to use a key (such as the *Observers Book of Rocks and Minerals*) to identify their rock samples. Soil, when mixed with water and allowed to settle, will settle out into layers of different sized particles (large stones at the bottom to fine clay at the top). Soil can be mixed with pre-boiled water and tested for acidity. Good gardening books will explain the importance of this to the horticulturist.

Comparing rocks and soils

Name _____ Date _____

Compare and describe the rocks or soils using your senses or simple tests.
How are they the same? How are they different?

Rock or soil sample	Appearance	Texture	My test results

Use a ruler to draw a line between each sample.

Heating and cooling

National Curriculum focus
Sc3/2b to describe changes that occur when materials are heated or cooled;
Sc3/2c that temperature is a measure of how hot or cold things are;
Sc3/2d about reversible changes, including dissolving, melting, boiling, condensing, freezing and evaporating.

Assessment objective
The children should demonstrate that they can identify and describe the changes caused to some common materials by heating and cooling them.

Potential assessment activities	Assessment outcomes
Children sort or order materials according to how they predict they might react on heating or cooling.	Children should be able to identify changes that can be reversed and those which cannot.
Through discussion (group or class), children describe how some materials change on heating and cooling.	Children should use appropriate vocabulary to describe the characteristics and processes.
Working in groups, children design simple tests to compare different materials as they are heated or cooled and make appropriate observations. Children describe the similarities and differences between a range of materials in terms of the changes that they go through and the reversibility of those changes (eg cooked food and boiled water).	Working in a practical situation, children should plan safe and simple tests to compare how different materials change on heating and cooling. Children should demonstrate their knowledge of a range of different materials and accurately identify the likely changes.
On the PCM children record, using a combination of drawings and text, their understanding of what happens to a material on heating and cooling.	Children should use appropriate vocabulary to accurately describe the process and changes.

Example of a child's response

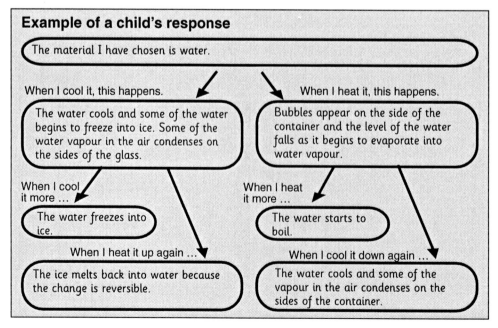

Key vocabulary
Boil
Condense
Evaporate
Freeze
Melt
Reversible

Heating and cooling

Name _____ Date _____

Choose a material. Draw it and explain how it might change when you heat it and cool it.
Use scientific words where you can, and say whether the change is reversible.

The material I have chosen is …

When I cool it, this happens.

When I heat it, this happens.

When I cool it more …

When I heat it more …

When I heat it up again …

When I cool it down again …

Mixing and separating

National Curriculum focus
Sc3/3a how to separate solid particles of different sizes by sieving;
Sc3/3b that some solids dissolve in water to give solutions;
Sc3/3c how to separate insoluble solids from liquids by filtering;
Sc3/3d how to recover dissolved solids by evaporating the liquid from the solution;
Sc3/3e to use knowledge of solids, liquids and gases to decide how mixtures might be separated.

Assessment objective
The children should demonstrate that they can describe what happens as particles of solids are mixed with and separated from water and other solid particles.

Potential assessment activities	Assessment outcomes
Children observe and describe what happens as they mix particles of food (rice, flour, salt, etc) with water.	Children should be able to recognize a solution and suspension.
Through discussion (group or class), children suggest ways in which the particles of food added to the water in the first activity could be recovered.	Children should use appropriate vocabulary to describe how they might separate mixtures (filter, sieve, evaporate).
Working in groups, children plan and carry out investigations focusing on factors which might affect the rate that (eg) salt dissolves in water.	Working in a practical situation, children should plan simple fair tests to be able to investigate (eg) amount and temperature of water, time, stirring, demonstrating that they can identify the important variables.
On the PCM children apply their understanding of mixing and separating of materials to particular situations.	Children should identify the appropriate scientific terminology to describe the mixing and separation procedures.

Example of a child's response

	What happens when the mix?	How would you try to separate them?	Adding more of the first substance
Salt into water	The salt dissolves	By evaporating the water	Too much salt will will leave a sediment at the bottom
Sand into water	Sand is suspended in water (for a very short time!)	Filtering	
Flour into water	The same as sand, but it takes longer to separate	Filtering	
Sugar into water	The sugar dissolves	By evaporating the water	Too much sugar will will leave a sediment at the bottom
Sand into rice		By sieving (filtration)	

Key vocabulary
Dissolve
Evaporate
Filter
Insoluble
Particles
Sediment
Soluble
Solution
Suspension

Mixing and separating

Show that you know what happens when substances are mixed together. Think about how you could separate these mixtures. Are you able to collect the original substances? Use the correct scientific words where you can.

Try out your ideas to see what happens.

	What happens when they mix?	How would you try to separate them?	What might happen if you tried to add more of the first substance?
salt into water			
sand into water			
flour into water			
sugar into water			
sand into rice			

Solids, liquids and gases

National Curriculum focus
Sc3/1e to recognize the differences between solids, liquids and gases, in terms of ease of flow and maintenance of shape and volume.

Assessment objective
The children should demonstrate that they can describe the differences between solids, liquids and gases.

Potential assessment activities	Assessment outcomes
Children sort a range of named substances into the three categories (it is easier to point to a 'coffee table' than define/describe what a table is).	Children should be able to place substances such as ice, rock, air into the appropriate groups.
Through discussion (group or class), children suggest definitions for the three states.	Children should use appropriate vocabulary to describe the similarities and differences between the three states.
Working in groups, children discuss the nature of substances such as clay (when it is in its mouldable form). It is a very stiff suspension of clay particles in water!	Children should recognize the difficulties in defining the nature of some materials and consider further their definitions.
Children produce a poster (drawn or using pictures from magazines) to exemplify the three states.	Children choose appropriate examples.
On the PCM children define and give examples of solids, liquids and gases.	Children should give appropriate definitions and examples of solids, liquids and gases. If the child's explanation refers correctly to the particulate nature of matter, this indicates that the child is working at a higher level.

Example of a child's response

Properties	Solids	Liquids	Gases
	A solid retains its shape, having a fixed internal structure.	Liquids flow and will adapt their shape to fill the base of a container to a common level. The particles of a liquid are attracted to each other but their positions are not fixed.	Gases disperse and flow to fill a container They need to be enclosed if they are to be kept. Sometimes they can be sensed by smell or sight.
Examples	rock, iron, wood, rubber, ...	water, milk, orange juice, tea, ...	air, water vapour, ...

Key vocabulary
Gas
Liquid
Particles
Solid

Solids, liquids and gases

Name _____ Date _____

Show what you know about solids, liquids and gases. What properties do they have? Can you think of examples of each?

Properties	Solids	Liquids	Gases
How can you tell that it is there? What shape does it take up? How do the bits that it is made up of move?			
Examples			
Can some substances be found as solids, liquids and gases? Which is the hardest list to write? Why?			

Water cycle

National Curriculum focus
Sc3/2e the part played by evaporation and condensation in the water cycle.

Assessment objective
The children should demonstrate that they can describe and explain the main features of the water cycle.

Potential assessment activities	Assessment outcomes
Children observe and describe what happens as a puddle evaporates.	Children should use appropriate vocabulary and sequence events correctly.
Through discussion (group or class), children suggest where the water from clouds comes from.	Children should be able to identify and use their own knowledge, particularly from empirical evidence, to offer a plausible hypothesis.
Working in groups, children research the water cycle and report back to the class. Children produce a poster (drawn or using pictures from magazines) to explain the water cycle.	Children should be able to identify the key features and go to an appropriate range of reference sources.
On the PCM children explain the water cycle, using drawings and appropriate scientific terminology.	Children should use appropriate scientific vocabulary when describing the sequence. Proper use of the terms evaporation, condensation and precipitation indicates that the child is working at a higher level.

Example of a child's response (words only)

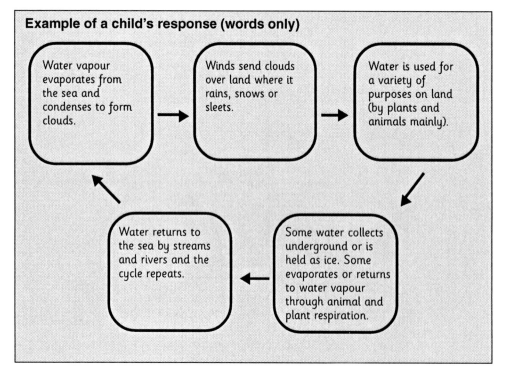

Key vocabulary
Air
Boil
Condense
Cycle
Evaporate
Freeze
Melt
Water vapour

Water cycle

Name _____ Date _____

Draw what you think happens during the water cycle.

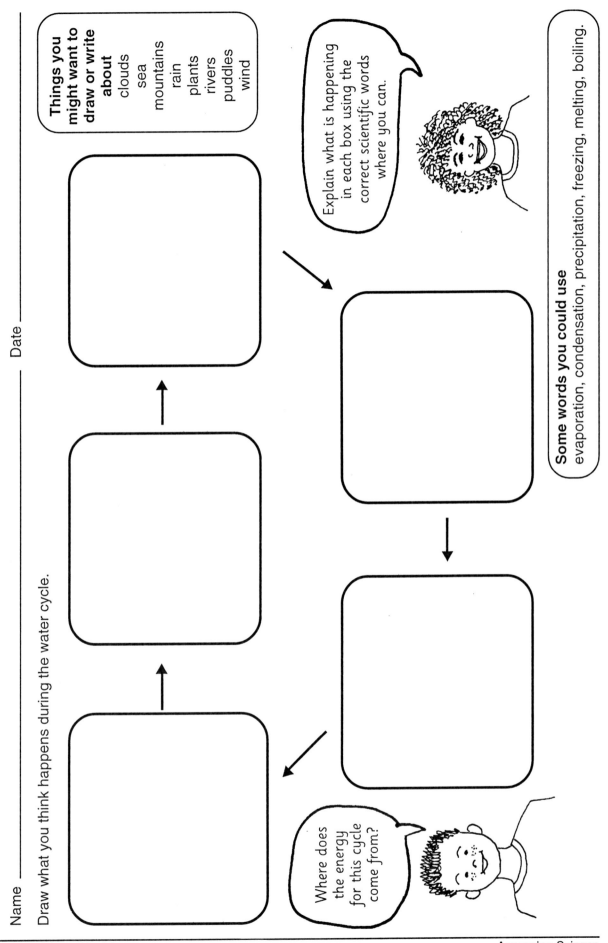

Things you might want to draw or write **about**

clouds
sea
mountains
rain
plants
rivers
puddles
wind

Explain what is happening in each box using the correct scientific words where you can.

Some words you could use
evaporation, condensation, precipitation, freezing, melting, boiling.

Where does the energy for this cycle come from?

Compression and tension

National Curriculum focus
Sc4/2d that when objects are pushed or pulled, an opposing pull or push can be felt;
Sc4/2e how to measure forces and identify the direction in which they act.

Assessment objective
The children should demonstrate that they can identify and explain the nature of compression and tension forces in a range of situations relating to elastic materials and objects.

Potential assessment activities	Assessment outcomes
Children investigate and describe compressing and stretching springs and elastic bands.	Children describe the 'push' of a stretched spring or 'pull' of an elasticated band as it attempts to revert to its original size and shape.
Through discussion (group or class), children identify a range of elastic materials or objects (springs, rubber bands and balls, elastic, upholstery foam, etc.) and relate this property to the potential uses.	Children should make a list of objects which can be squashed or stretched but will revert to their original shapes/sizes when released.
In a group, children sort a range of toys (or pictures of common moving objects) to identify those where compression/tension forces are used either within the materials or the mechanism.	Children should describe, either verbally or using writing/drawings, how compression or tension forces are used in each example they identify.
On the PCM children explain how compression/ tension forces are applied in particular given circumstances.	Children should recognize the direction of a force being exerted by a spring in terms of a compression or extension.

Example of a child's response

The force of the rubber ball hitting the floor makes the ball compress. It then springs back to its original shape, pushing against the floor and 'bouncing'.

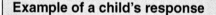

The spring in the pop-up toy is kept compressed by the sucker holding it down. When the force of the spring finally pushes open the sucker, the whole toy jumps into the air.

When the pull stretching the rubber band is released, the band shortens pulling the paper dart into the air.

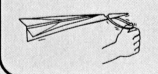

The bird is pulled down to place the spring under tension. When the bird is let go, the spring contracts, pulling the bird up. Gravity pulls the bird down which stretches the spring again. The bird will bounce up and down under the effects of gravity and tension in the spring. The bounce will get smaller each time until it stops.

Key vocabulary
Compression
Elastic
Gravity
Tension

Compression and tension

Name _____ Date _____

Elastic materials or objects can be squashed or stretched by forces acting on them.
Try to explain how and where the forces are acting in these drawings.

A rubber ball bouncing on the floor

A spring 'powered' pop-up toy

A paper dart launched with a rubber band

A bouncing 'bird-on-a-spring'

Frictional forces

National Curriculum focus

Sc4/2c about friction, including air resistance, as a force which slows moving objects and may prevent objects from starting to move;

Sc4/2e how to measure forces and identify the direction in which they act.

Assessment objective

The children should demonstrate that they can identify and describe the effect of frictional forces within a range of situations.

Potential assessment activities	Assessment outcomes
Children identify and describe what a 'force' is.	Children should be able to identify forces in terms of push, pull and twist.
Through discussion (group or class), children describe a number of different situations where movement is restricted by the application of frictional forces.	Children should recognize friction as a force that restricts movement.
Working in groups, children describe and model situations where friction has both beneficial and detrimental effects. Children explain, as a group, the sources and effects of friction in different situations.	Children should be able to identify situations where the frictional force is either preventing an object from moving in the first place (providing grip) or slowing a moving object (a resistant force opposite to the direction of movement).
On the PCM children explain, through drawings and written explanations, the nature and effects of friction in given situations.	Children should be able to use vocabulary and force arrows effectively and accurately.

Example of a child's response

There is a frictional force acting between the surfaces of the table and book against the direction of movement. Lubricants can reduce surface friction.

friction

gravity

As things fall, air gets in the way and stops them from falling any faster. A parachute makes more air get in the way and makes the thing fall more slowly than it would have done. The air resistance is a friction force.

friction

gravity

There is friction between the shoe and the surface of the slope. Without sufficient grip the person would slide back down the slope due to the pull of gravity. The friction is acting in the direction of the slope (upwards). The friction would be less by having less grip on the sole of the shoes or having a slippery, ice or muddy surface.

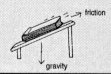

friction

gravity

The toy is slowing to a stop. Once the push to set the toy in motion is finished, frictional forces, both between the surface and the wheels and the axles and the axle holders, slow the lorry until it stops. A smooth surface and lubricated axle holders will reduce friction letting the lorry to roll further.

surface pushing up

gravity

friction

Key vocabulary

Air resistance
Force
Friction
Gravity
Grip
Lubrication
Thrust

Frictional forces

Name _____ Date _____

Friction slows moving objects. Try to explain where the friction is in each of these cases. Draw arrows to show which way the force acts. How can the effect of friction be reduced?

A book sliding across a table

A package falling with a parachute

A person walking up a steep slope

A toy rolling across the floor

Balanced/unbalanced forces

National Curriculum focus

Sc4/2b that objects are pulled downwards because of the gravitational attraction between them and the Earth;

Sc4/2c about friction, including air resistance, as a force that slows moving objects and may prevent objects from starting to move.

Assessment objective

The children should demonstrate that they can identify situations where balanced and unbalanced forces are interacting and describe the effect.

Potential assessment activities	Assessment outcomes
Children identify and describe what a 'force' is.	Children should be able to identify forces in terms of push, pull and twist.
Through discussion (group or class), children describe a number of different situations, identifying where forces are involved.	They should be able to describe situations where pushes, pulls and twists are used.
Working in groups, children describe and model situations involving balanced and unbalanced forces. Children explain the difference between balanced and unbalanced force systems.	Children should be able to identify situations where there is a change in motion (direction or speed) as 'unbalanced' and where there is no change in motion (stationary or constant speed and direction) as 'balanced'.
On the PCM children explain, through drawings and written explanations, the nature of the forces in a given situation.	Children should use appropriate vocabulary and the force arrows should be correctly proportioned and positioned.

Example of a child's response

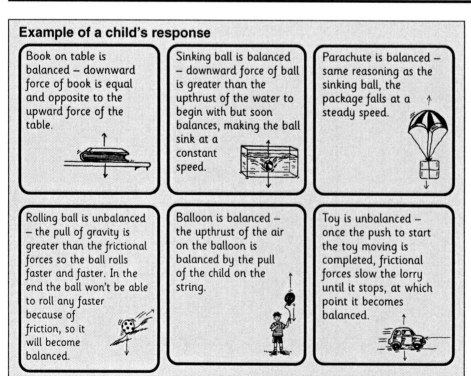

Book on table is balanced – downward force of book is equal and opposite to the upward force of the table.

Sinking ball is balanced – downward force of ball is greater than the upthrust of the water to begin with but soon balances, making the ball sink at a constant speed.

Parachute is balanced – same reasoning as the sinking ball, the package falls at a steady speed.

Rolling ball is unbalanced – the pull of gravity is greater than the frictional forces so the ball rolls faster and faster. In the end the ball won't be able to roll any faster because of friction, so it will become balanced.

Balloon is balanced – the upthrust of the air on the balloon is balanced by the pull of the child on the string.

Toy is unbalanced – once the push to start the toy moving is completed, frictional forces slow the lorry until it stops, at which point it becomes balanced.

Key vocabulary

Balanced forces
Unbalanced forces
Upthrust

Balanced/unbalanced forces

Name _____ Date _____

Forces acting upon an object can be said to be either balanced or unbalanced.
Try to explain what is happening in each of these cases.
Draw arrows to show which way the forces act.

A package falling with a
parachute is _____

because …

A toy rolling across the floor
is _____

because …

A ball slowly sinking in a
tank of water is _____

because …

A child holding a balloon in
the air is _____

because …

A book resting on a table is _____

because…

A ball starting to roll down
a slope is _____

because …

Magnets and magnetic materials

National Curriculum focus
Sc4/2a   about the forces of attraction and repulsion between magnets, and about the forces of attraction between magnets and magnetic materials.

Assessment objective
The children should demonstrate that they can describe the various different properties of magnets and magnetic materials.

Potential assessment activities	Assessment outcomes
Children sort materials using a magnet.	Children should be able to identify the metals which are attracted to the magnet.
Children use a magnetic compass to find magnetic north.	Children should realize that the Earth has a magnetic field.
Children describe what happens when two magnets are brought together. Children design and carry out an investigation to test the strength of a magnet.	Working in a practical situation, children should design and construct appropriate illustrative or investigative activities.
On the PCM children explain, through drawings and written explanations, the nature and effects of the properties of a magnet.	Children should use the correct vocabulary appropriately.

Key vocabulary
Attraction
Magnetic
Repulsion

Example of a child's response

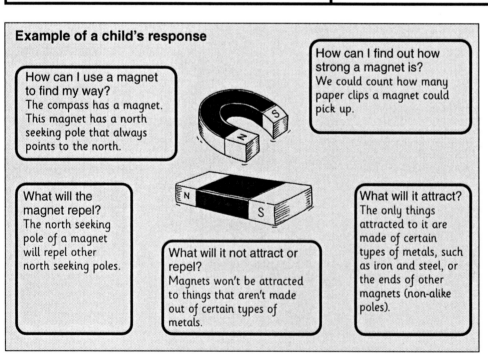

How can I use a magnet to find my way?
The compass has a magnet. This magnet has a north seeking pole that always points to the north.

How can I find out how strong a magnet is?
We could count how many paper clips a magnet could pick up.

What will the magnet repel?
The north seeking pole of a magnet will repel other north seeking poles.

What will it not attract or repel?
Magnets won't be attracted to things that aren't made out of certain types of metals.

What will it attract?
The only things attracted to it are made of certain types of metals, such as iron and steel, or the ends of other magnets (non-alike poles).

Magnets and magnetic materials

Name _____

Date _____

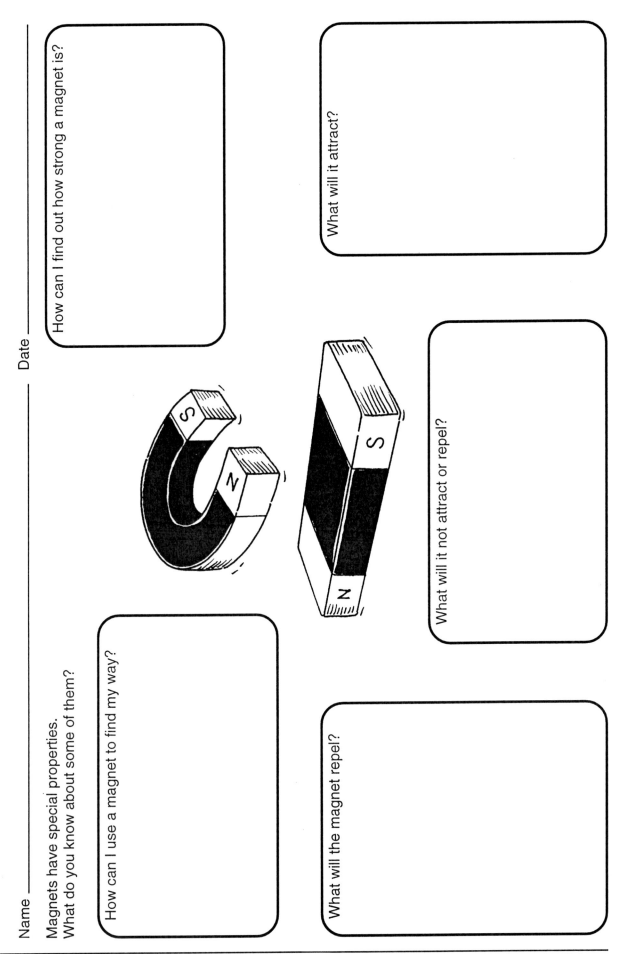

How can I find out how strong a magnet is?

What will it attract?

What will it not attract or repel?

Magnets have special properties.
What do you know about some of them?

How can I use a magnet to find my way?

What will the magnet repel?

Making circuits

National Curriculum focus

Sc4/1a to construct circuits, incorporating a battery or power supply and a range of switches, to make electrical devices work;

Sc4/1c how to represent series circuits by drawings and conventional symbols, and how to construct series circuits on the basis of drawings and diagrams using conventional symbols.

Assessment objective

The children should demonstrate that they can identify electrical component symbols and use them to draw appropriate circuits.

Potential assessment activities	Assessment outcomes
Children construct simple electrical circuits.	Children should know that a complete circuit is necessary for the components to work and the position of the terminals on those components.
Children identify a range of circuit symbols on the PCM.	Children should identify the circuit symbols correctly (see 'Example of a child's response').
Working individually or in groups, children design and construct circuits to perform particular tasks. Children record their circuits in the form of circuit diagrams on the PCM. Children produce circuits, working from given circuit diagrams.	Children should be able to correctly identify the symbols and use them appropriately in designing the necessary circuits.

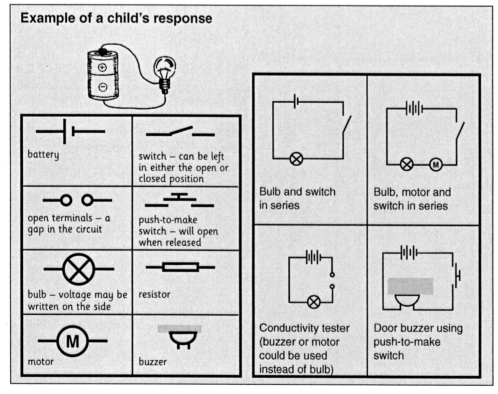

Example of a child's response

battery

switch – can be left in either the open or closed position

open terminals – a gap in the circuit

push-to-make switch – will open when released

bulb – voltage may be written on the side

resistor

motor

buzzer

Bulb and switch in series

Bulb, motor and switch in series

Conductivity tester (buzzer or motor could be used instead of bulb)

Door buzzer using push-to-make switch

Key vocabulary

Battery
Bulb
Buzzer
Circuit
Motor
Parallel
Resistor
Series
Switch
Terminal

Note

The symbol for a battery denotes a 1.5V cell. To indicate, eg a 4.5V battery, either three 1.5V cells can be shown, or the voltage can be written on top as follows:

45V

Making circuits

Name _____ Date _____

Draw connecting wires from the battery to the bulb to complete the circuit.

Draw these circuits using the appropriate symbols.

A 1.5V circuit with a bulb and switch in series.	A 4.5V circuit with a bulb, motor and switch in series.

A 4.5V circuit to test the conductivity of materials.	A 4.5V circuit to operate as a door buzzer.

Check that the circuits work by making them.

Explain what these circuit symbols mean.

Brighter and dimmer

National Curriculum focus
Sc4/1b how changing the number or type of components in a series circuit can make bulbs brighter or dimmer;
Sc4/1c how to represent series circuits by drawings and conventional symbols, and how to construct series circuits on the basis of drawings and diagrams using conventional symbols.

Assessment objective
The children should demonstrate that they can identify different ways of increasing and reducing the amount of light produced by an electrical circuit.

Potential assessment activities	Assessment outcomes
Children identify situations where the amount of electricity or the effect of that electricity in a circuit needs to be varied.	Children should be able to identify the importance of changing the amount of light, heat, movement or sound produced by an electrical device.
Through discussion (group or class), children describe a number of different situations where the speed, brightness or heat produced by an electrical device is varied.	Children should identify situations such as lighting (dimmer switches, change the bulb or battery); movement (food mixer, radio controlled car); heat (hair drier, toaster); sound (radio).
Working in groups, children design circuits to change the output of an electrical device. Children explain how these circuits change the output of the device.	Working in a practical situation, children should be able to design and construct appropriate circuits, explaining their reasoning.
On the PCM children explain, through drawings and written explanations, the nature and effects of changes to a circuit which will affect the output of an electrical device.	Children should provide realistic methods for increasing and reducing the brightness of the light, using appropriate vocabulary.

Example of a child's response (words only)

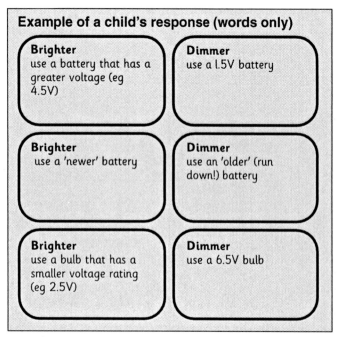

Brighter
use a battery that has a greater voltage (eg 4.5V)

Dimmer
use a 1.5V battery

Brighter
use a 'newer' battery

Dimmer
use an 'older' (run down!) battery

Brighter
use a bulb that has a smaller voltage rating (eg 2.5V)

Dimmer
use a 6.5V bulb

Key vocabulary
Device

Notes
Another way of making the light brighter is to connect two 3.5V bulbs in parallel.

Other ways of making the light dimmer include:
*   connect another device (eg motor, buzzer, resistor) in series with the bulb;
*   use a variable resistor to 'turn the bulb down';
*   connect a 'poor' conducting material (eg pencil lead) into the circuit.

Brighter and dimmer

Name _____ Date _____

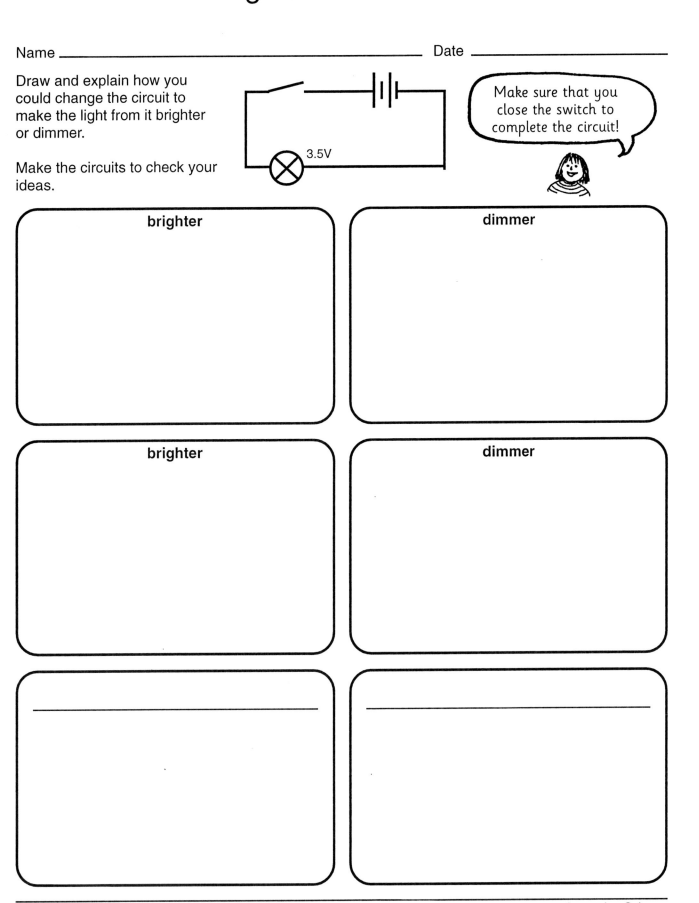

Draw and explain how you could change the circuit to make the light from it brighter or dimmer.

Make the circuits to check your ideas.

3.5V

Make sure that you close the switch to complete the circuit!

brighter

dimmer

brighter

dimmer

Controlling electrical devices

National Curriculum focus

Sc4/1a to construct circuits, incorporating a battery or power supply and a range of switches, to make electrical devices work.

Assessment objective

The children should demonstrate that they can choose appropriate switches and place them within a circuit to produce the required effect.

Potential assessment activities	Assessment outcomes
Through discussion (group or class), children describe a number of different situations where and why different types of switches are used.	Children should be able to identify switches in common pieces of electrical equipment and explain that these switches break and make the circuit allowing the electricity to flow.
Working individually or in groups, children construct circuits making appropriate use of switches.	Children should be able to demonstrate understanding of switching systems through their choice and positioning of switches.
Children design and make circuits shown on PCM explaining, as appropriate, the use of particular switches to control different components as required.	Children should demonstrate an understanding of how switches work.

Key vocabulary
Parallel
Series
Twin pole switch

Example of a child's response

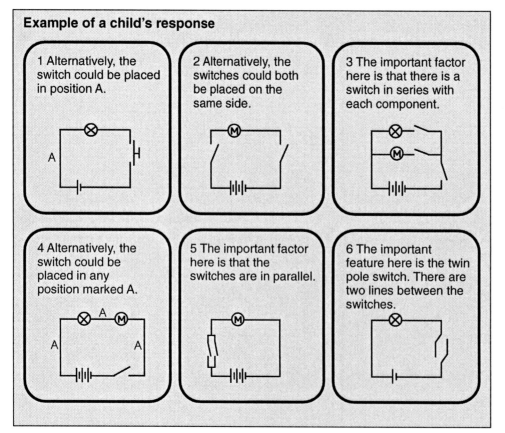

1 Alternatively, the switch could be placed in position A.

2 Alternatively, the switches could both be placed on the same side.

3 The important factor here is that there is a switch in series with each component.

4 Alternatively, the switch could be placed in any position marked A.

5 The important factor here is that the switches are in parallel.

6 The important feature here is the twin pole switch. There are two lines between the switches.

Controlling electrical devices

Draw and explain how you would place and use switches to control these circuits.
Construct the circuits to check your ideas.

Hint: here are two types of switches you could use.

Switch symbol

Push-to-make switch symbol

1   Use a switch that will not allow the bulb to be left on when it is unattended.

2   Use two switches connected so that they both have to be on for the motor to work.

3   Use three switches connected so that one is a 'master' switch controlling both and each component has its own switch.

4   Use a switch that will control the motor and the bulb at the same time. How many different places could you put it?

5   Use two switches connected so that either or both can be on for the motor to work.

6   Design a switching system that allows the bulb to be turned on or off from either switch (like the light at the top of a set of stairs).

Properties of light

National Curriculum focus
Sc4/3a   that light travels from a source;
Sc4/3b   that light cannot pass through some materials and how this leads to the formation of shadows;
Sc4/3c   that light is reflected from surfaces;
Sc4/3d   that we see things only when light from them enters our eyes.

Assessment objective
The children should demonstrate that they can describe some of the transmission and reflective properties of light.

Potential assessment activities	Assessment outcomes
Through discussion (group or class), children describe how they are able to see light sources and other objects.Working in groups, children draw diagrams to show how light travels from a source via objects to their eyes.	Children should be able to identify that light travels in straight lines.
By reference to examples, children explain the difference between opaque, translucent and transparent materials.	Children should use their understanding of the nature of light to explain the production of shadows.
On the PCM children explain, through drawings and written explanations, the nature and effects of light travelling from a source to their eyes.	Children should be able to use their understanding of reflection to explain why a periscope works and to draw the path taken by the light. They should be able to explain how light passes through transparent and translucent materials, but not through opaque materials.

Key vocabulary
Opaque
Translucent
Transparent

Example of a child's response

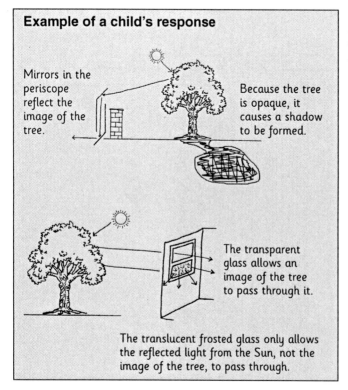

Mirrors in the periscope reflect the image of the tree.

Because the tree is opaque, it causes a shadow to be formed.

The transparent glass allows an image of the tree to pass through it.

The translucent frosted glass only allows the reflected light from the Sun, not the image of the tree, to pass through.

Properties of light

Name _____ Date _____

Use lines with arrows and words to describe and explain what happens to the light coming from the Sun and how this light enables us to see things. Try to use scientific words where you can.

Use words and pictures to explain how you can see the tree when you look through the windows.

Days, months and years

National Curriculum focus

Sc4/4c   how day and night are related to the spin of the Earth on its own axis;

Sc4/4d   that the Earth orbits the Sun once each year, and that the Moon takes approximately 28 days to orbit the Earth.

Assessment objective

The children should demonstrate that they can describe and explain the astronomical motion that leads to the defining of 'day', 'month' and 'year'.

Potential assessment activities	Assessment outcomes
Children can be asked to identify and name different time periods.	Children should identify the 'natural' time periods, eg the seasons, along with artificial ones such as hour, second and minute.
Through discussion (group or class), children identify a number of different solar bodies.	Children should identify the Sun and planets within the solar system.
Working in groups, children describe and model the motions of solar bodies. Children describe, as a group, how the motion of solar bodies links to the definition of units of time.	Children should explain the motions of solar bodies in terms of orbits and rotations; that these are regular; and that they are used as a basis for the measurement of time periods.
On the PCM children explain, through drawings and written explanations, day, month and year in terms of the relative motion of the Sun, Earth and Moon.	Children should use the correct vocabulary to describe the relative motions and give accurate approximations of the time periods.

Example of a child's response

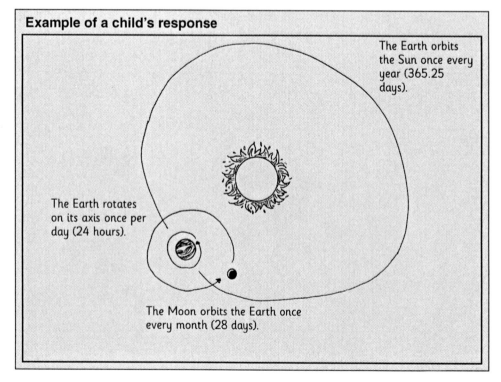

The Earth orbits the Sun once every year (365.25 days).

The Earth rotates on its axis once per day (24 hours).

The Moon orbits the Earth once every month (28 days).

Key vocabulary
Asteroid
Axis
Orbit
Planet
Rotation
Satellite (moon)
Solar system
Star
Sun

Days, months and years

Name _____

Date _____

Add to the drawing below and use words to explain how we measure days, months and years.

Time of day/time of year

National Curriculum focus
Sc4/4b how the position of the Sun appears to change during the day, and how shadows change as this happens.

Assessment objective
The children should demonstrate that they can identify and explain the daily and seasonal changes in the position and inclination of the Sun.

Potential assessment activities	Assessment outcomes
Children experience and describe the shape and position of their own shadows on a sunny day.	Children should recognize that the shadows are on the opposite side of them to the Sun; their shadows are the same 'shape' as them; and that the shadows are 'attached' to them.
Through discussion (group or class), children explain how the position of the Sun and shadows change during the day. In a group, children should observe and record the position of the Sun with the length and direction of a shadow (eg of a tree).	Children should identify the east-to-west traversing of the Sun across the sky and the changing position of shadows as a consequence, noting that the Sun reaches its highest inclination around midday. Also that the higher the Sun is, the shorter the shadow for any given object is.
Children discuss, in a group, the seasonal changes to the position of the Sun. On the PCM children link the daily and seasonal changes to the position of the Sun to the shadows that are produced.	Children should identify that although the direction of the Sun will be the same at any given time during the year, its inclination will change. It will be highest in the summer and lowest in winter. Some children may note the change in position due to the changes to and from BST and GMT.

Key vocabulary
Season
Shadow

Example of a child's response

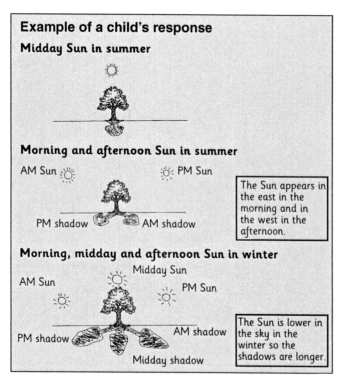

Time of day/time of year

Name _____ Date _____

It is midday in the summer. Draw the shadow caused by the tree.

Draw and explain where the Sun and the shadows would be in the morning and afternoon in the summer.

Draw and explain what would happen at the same times of the day in the winter.

Changing sounds

National Curriculum focus
Sc4/3f   how to change the pitch and loudness of sounds produced by some vibrating objects.

Assessment objective
The children should demonstrate that they can identify and explain how the sound made by a musical instrument can be changed.

Potential assessment activities	Assessment outcomes
Children examine tunable musical instruments in order to identify, demonstrate and describe how the sound can be changed.	Children should compare instruments and link the notes produced with the physical differences, eg length, type, thickness and tightness of string.
In a group, children sort a range of musical instruments into groups by the method of tuning that they employ. They explain how the different methods work.	Children should categorize correctly the instruments and verbally explain how the sounds are changed.
Individually, children explain how a simple stringed musical instrument can be altered to produce different sounds.	Children should be able to describe through drawings or verbally how the different sounds can be produced.
Children carry out an investigation to establish the effect of changing one tuning factor on the note produced by a simple table top guitar and record their response on the PCM (a bottle xylophone could be used instead).	Children should be able to identify several different options (eg type, thickness, length, tightness of string) and use these to plan a fair test investigation.

Key vocabulary
Amplitude
Pitch
Timbre
Vibration

Example of a child's response (words only)

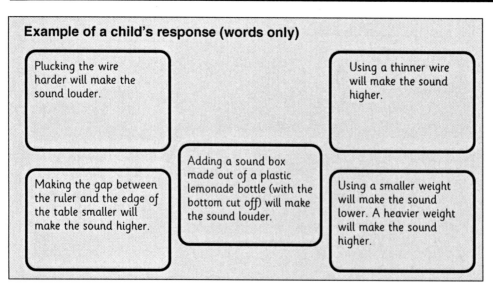

Plucking the wire harder will make the sound louder.

Using a thinner wire will make the sound higher.

Making the gap between the ruler and the edge of the table smaller will make the sound higher.

Adding a sound box made out of a plastic lemonade bottle (with the bottom cut off) will make the sound louder.

Using a smaller weight will make the sound lower. A heavier weight will make the sound higher.

Notes
Each type of instrument will have its own particular differences but generally, no matter how an instrument makes a sound, doing it harder will make it louder (increased volume or amplitude). The longer or thicker (generally bigger!) the part of the instrument that makes the sound (string, tube, skin,...), the lower the note it produces will be (lower pitch). In the case of instruments using stretched strings or skins (eg banjo, drum) the tighter they are stretched the higher the note will be (higher pitch).

Changing sounds

If you pluck a stringed instrument, what things can you do to change the sound that it makes? Draw some of them. Explain what is happening.

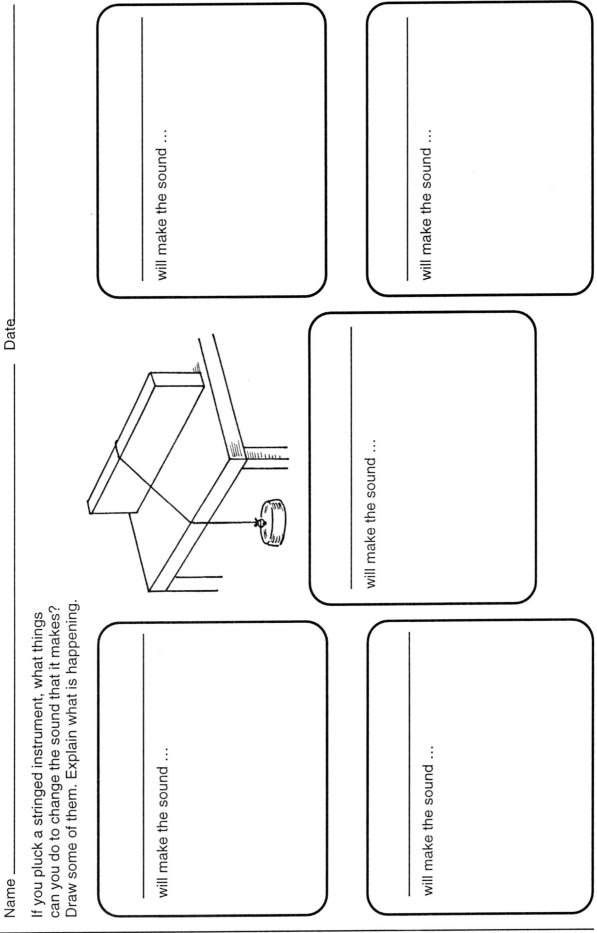

will make the sound …

will make the sound …

will make the sound …

will make the sound …

will make the sound …

Sounds all around

National Curriculum focus
Sc4/3e that sounds are made when objects vibrate but that vibrations are not always directly visible.

Assessment objective
The children should demonstrate that they can identify and explain how sounds are made and transmitted via vibrations.

Potential assessment activities	Assessment outcomes
Children experience and describe the sounds made by a variety of musical instruments.	Children describe the sound production in terms of 'blowing', 'hitting', 'scraping', 'plucking' and 'shaking'.
Through discussion (group or class), children identify how particular instruments produce sounds.	Children should be able to describe, sort and categorize the instruments according to the different types of sound production.
In a group, children sort a range of musical instruments into groups by the method of sound production.	Children should physically be able to place instruments into sets.
Children discuss, in a group, the different methods of sound production and identify examples of instruments using each.	Children should be able to identify differences within categories (eg woodwind, brass, etc).
On the PCM children explain how different instruments produce sound.	Children should explain sound production in terms of vibrations.

Example of a child's response (words only)

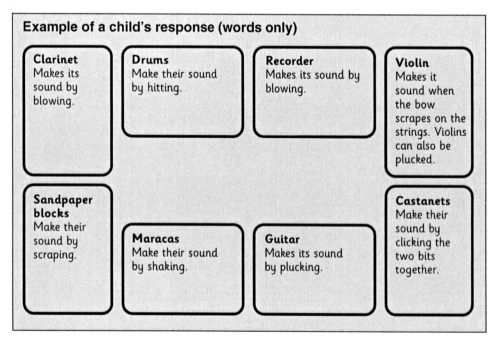

Clarinet
Makes its sound by blowing.

Drums
Make their sound by hitting.

Recorder
Makes its sound by blowing.

Violin
Makes it sound when the bow scrapes on the strings. Violins can also be plucked.

Sandpaper blocks
Make their sound by scraping.

Maracas
Make their sound by shaking.

Guitar
Makes its sound by plucking.

Castanets
Make their sound by clicking the two bits together.

Key vocabulary
Vibration

Note
Children may also identify electronic keyboards and similar instruments – these rely on sound production through a loudspeaker (usually a vibrating paper cone).

Sounds all around

Name _____ Date _____

Different musical instruments make sounds in different ways.
Draw some of them. How do they make sounds?

Write down what each instrument is and how the sound is made next to your drawings.

Teachers' glossary of scientific terms

Please note that this list is by no means exhaustive and should be used as a guide. Terms marked * are more appropriate for children working with the Key Stage 3 Programme of Study. It must also be noted that only knowing a word is insufficient. Children need to be able to use this vocabulary appropriately and at least have some understanding of the concepts behind them.

Absorbent
Describes a material, object or body which can take in or 'suck up' another (eg sponge *absorbs* water).

Air
Mixture of gases (mainly nitrogen and oxygen) which we breathe in.

Air resistance
Friction caused by movement through air.

Amphibian
An animal with a backbone which can breathe both in air and in water.

Amplitude*
Effectively the volume of the sound, how loud it is. Distance between the peak and trough of a vibration when pictured as a wave form.

Antagonistic pair
A pair of muscles so arranged that one will reverse the body part movement of the other.

Anther
The part of the flower head which contains pollen.

Arteries
Vessels which transport blood away from the heart.

Asteroid
A 'small' body which orbits around a star.

Attraction
The force between a magnet and a magnetic material.

Axis
The line about which a rotating body spins (eg a planet).

Balanced forces
Here the forces applied to an object leave it stationary, or moving at a constant speed in the same direction.

Battery
A series of cells which store electricity chemically.

Blood
The fluid in the heart, veins and arteries which carries oxygen round the body.

Boil
To change from a liquid to a gaseous state due to heating (water to steam).

Bone
One of the hard parts of a body which all together make a skeleton.

Brain
The organ inside the skull which controls the body.

Breathe
Take air into and expel it from the lungs.

Bulb
An electrical device which turns electricity into light and some heat.

Buzzer
A device that makes a buzzing sound.

Camouflage
Colouring that hides animals, vehicles or people by blending them into their background.

Canine
Pointed teeth situated between the incisors and the first premolar.

Capillaries
Very fine blood vessels.

Carbohydrates
Sugars and starches found in food which give energy.

Carbon dioxide*
The gas used in photosynthesis. It is more prevalent in exhaled air and in combustion.

Carnivore
Animal that feeds on other animals.

Circuit
A pathway for electricity to flow.

Climate
The normal weather conditions of a particular area.

Combustion*
Burning process where oxygen is required and carbon dioxide and water are produced.

Compression
Where a force is applied to 'squash' an object.

Condense
To change from a gaseous to a liquid state due to cooling.

Cycle
A continuous and recurrent process.

Decant*
To separate two substances by pouring off the top layer.

Decomposers
Plants and animals which help dead organic matter to biodegrade.

Dentine
Hard dense tissue which forms main part of teeth.

Device (electricity)
An active component in an electrical circuit, eg bulb, motor buzzer, resistor.

Diet
One's habitual food.

Digestion
When food is digested, it is passed through the stomach where it is broken down to provide energy.

Dispersal
To disperse is to become spread widely.

Dissolve
To mix one substance into another so that they can only be reclaimed through evaporation or distillation (eg salt in water).

Distil*
To separate the solvent from a solution through evaporation (eg collect the water from brine).

Drugs
Medical substances, used alone or as ingredients.

Ecosystem
Self-contained biological system consisting of the animals and plants living within a particular habitat including the energy input (the Sun).

Elastic
Describes a material or object which will return to its original shape after a compression or tension force has been removed.

Electrical conductor
Describes a material which allows electricity to flow through it.

Enamel
The hard white surface of your teeth.

Environment
The natural world – all the land, sea, plants and animals that live on the Earth.

Evaporate
To change from a liquid to a gaseous state (water to vapour).

Exercise
Exertion of muscles, limbs etc, especially for heath's sake.

Fats
Energy providing food group, found in food such as meat, milk and cheese.
Fibre
A part of food found in bran etc which the body cannot digest. Fibre encourages the intestines to work.
Filament*
Tube which supports the anther.
Filter
To separate a mixture by capturing the larger particles (often with a sieve).
Flower
Part of the plant usually made up of coloured petals.
Force
Amount of power used to move something.
Freeze
To change from a liquid to a solid state due to cooling.
Friction
A force which acts against the direction of movement to restrict or prevent movement.

Gas
A substance like air, neither liquid nor solid.
Germination
The point at which a dormant seed begins to grow.
Gravity
The force of attraction between two bodies (one needs to be massive for it to be noticeable).
Grip
A restraining force, usually a surface characteristic (increases the frictional force).
Grow
To develop and/or increase in size.
Gums
The firm pink flesh round the teeth.

Habitat
The natural home of a plant or animal.
Hard
Describes a material that is resistant to scratching.
Heart
The organ in the chest that pumps blood round the body.
Herbivore
Animal that feeds on plants.

Igneous*
Rock formed by the cooling and solidifying of magma (molten rock).
Incisors
The front teeth between the canine teeth.

Insoluble
Describes a substance, or part of a substance, that does not dissolve.
Intestine
Digestive tube after the stomach where nutrients are extracted from food.
Invertebrate
(Usually) small animal without a backbone.

Joint
The place where two bones join.

Kidneys
Organs which filter and remove waste from the body.

Leaf
One of the green, flat growths on trees or plants.
Liquid
A substance which is not solid and can flow.
Lubrication
Use of a substance between two surfaces to reduce friction (eg oil).
Lungs
The two organs inside the chest that fill up with air during breathing.

Magnetic
Describes a metal which is attracted to magnets.
Melt
To change from a solid to a liquid state due to heating.
Metamorphic*
Rock which has been subjected to great pressure and heat within the earth making it denser and harder than it originally was.
Micro-organism
Very small living thing (virus, bacteria).
Minerals
Substances which are found naturally in rocks and earth.
Molars
The wide teeth at the back of the mouth.
Molecule*
Smallest particle of a substance that can exist.
Moon
See Satellite.
Motor
A rotating machine that converts electrical energy into mechanical energy.
Muscles
Bundles of fibres connected to the bones of the body which enable people or animals to move.

Nutrient
A nutritious substance or ingredient.
Nutrition
Supplying or receiving of nourishment, food.

Omnivore
Animal that feeds on plants and other animals.
Opaque
Describes a material which does not allow light through it (ie produces a shadow).
Orbit
The circular or elliptical path taken by one astronomical body (planet, moon, asteroid, etc) around another (more massive) body (eg Earth around the Sun, Moon around the Earth).
Oxygen
Colourless, tasteless gas, existing in air – essential to animal and plant life.

Parallel (electricity)
Where components are connected allowing the electricity to take a choice of alternative pathways.
Particles
Very small bits of a substance.
Permeable
Describes the degree to which water can 'soak in' to a substance.
Petal
The coloured or white, leaf-like part of a flower that grows out from the centre.
Photosynthesis
Process by which green plants use energy from the Sun to break carbon dioxide into carbon and oxygen. The carbon is retained in the plant for food and the oxygen is returned to the atmosphere.
Pitch
The rate of vibration. The faster the vibration, the higher the pitch of the note.
Planet
A large body which orbits around a star (eg Earth about the Sun) which does not emit light.
Plastic
Describes a material which retains its shape, but also used to describe a particular group of synthetic materials (eg clay is plastic but not a plastic).
Pollen
Fertilizing powder produced by the flower of a plant.
Pollination
Process in which plants reproduce.
Predator
Animal that captures and feeds on other animals.

Premolars
Teeth in front of true molars.
Prey
Animal that is captured by and fed upon by other animals.
Primary producer
Plant that produces its own food using energy from the Sun.
Protein
'Body building' food group.
Pulp
Nervous substance in interior cavity of tooth.

Reproduce
To produce further members of same species by natural means.
Reptile
Air breathing vertebrate animal, normally egg laying, which relies on external sources of heat to control body temperature.
Repulsion
The force which pushes apart like poles on two magnets.
Resistor
Device having resistance to passage of current.
Rest
Absence of exertion, activity or movement.
Reversible
Describes a process which can go in either direction.
Rigid
Describes a material that is resistant to bending (flexibility).
Roots
The part of a plant that grows underground.
Rotation
The movement of a body about its axis.

Saliva
Colourless liquid secreted into mouth from salivary glands.
Satellite (or moon)
A small body which orbits around a planet (eg Moon about the Earth).
Season
Division of the year with distinguishable characteristics of temperature, rainfall, vegetation, etc.
Sediment
Solid particles that sometimes settle at the bottom of a liquid.
Sedimentary*
Rock that has been formed in layers usually from deposits of particles of eroded rock or organic material.
Sepal
One of the divisions of leaves forming the outer case of the flower bud.

Series (electricity)
Consecutive connection of components in a single loop to the power source.
Shadow
Region not reached by light because of intervening object.
Skeleton
The framework of bones that supports the muscles and organs inside humans and other animals.
Solar system
Those planets, asteroids and moons which orbit around a Sun.
Solid
A substance that retains its shape, having a fixed internal structure.
Soluble
Describes a substance which will mix evenly with a liquid so that particles can no longer be seen.
Solute*
A substance which can be added to a liquid and will dissolve in it.
Solution
A substance that is a mixture of solvent and solute.
Solvent*
The liquid that the substance has been dissolved in.
Stamen
The combined name for the anther and filament.
Star
An astronomical body which emits light (eg the Sun).
Stem
The long vertical part of a plant, supporting the leaves and flowers.
Stigma
The part of the flower head which receives pollen.
Stomach
The organ of the body in which food is digested before moving on to the intestines.
Strong
Describes a material or object which resists changes of shape caused by forces.
Style
Narrow tube between the ovary and stigma in a flower head through which the pollen moves.
Sun
The star that the Earth travels round and receives warmth and light from.
Suspension
Mixture in which the particles may be separated by filtration or sieving.
Switch
A device which you move to turn something on or off.

Teeth
The hard white objects in the mouth which are used to chew or bite food.
Tension
Where a force is applied to 'stretch' an object.
Terminal
One of the two places on a battery for wires to be attached.
Thermal insulator
Does not allow heat to flow through it easily.
Thrust
Push.
Timbre
The qualities of a sound which enables you to distinguish between the same notes produced by (eg) both a flute and a violin.
Translucent
Describes a material which allows light but not images through it.
Transparent
Describes a material which allows light and images through it.
Twin pole switch
Two switches connected with parallel lines, enabling either switch to connect the circuit.

Unbalanced forces
Where the force applied to an object causes it to accelerate, decelerate or change direction.
Upthrust
Upward force of water on a floating object.

Valve
Device which controls the flow of liquids or gases.
Veins
Vessels which transport blood to the heart.
Vertebrates
All animals with backbones.
Vibration
A rapid backwards and forwards movement (in the case of sound, this movement will cause compression waves to travel through air which can be sensed by our ears).
Vitamins
Organic s-ubstances essential in small quantities for good health.

Water vapour
Very small molecules of water usually in the air; gaseous state of water.

Do you have any slower learners in your science class?

Photocopiable

If so, you are probably used to modifying worksheets to suit their needs. The Brilliant Support Activities series has been specially written for slower learners and pupils with special needs, saving you time!

◆ Over 40 photocopiable worksheets in each book
◆ Written in simple language
◆ Encourages written responses to develop writing skills
◆ Clear, easy to understand line drawings
◆ Activities reinforce skills of observation, prediction, recording and drawing conclusions
◆ Paper-based and hands-on activities

Make Science Fun for you and your Pupils!

If you'd like exciting new ideas to put a buzz into your science lessons – look no further!

The Project Science Series for KS1 and KS2

- ◆ Brings key learning objectives to life in a way pupils will enjoy
- ◆ Contains creative, attention-grabbing, science lessons
- ◆ Comprehensive coverage of the 2000 National Curriculum for 5–11 year olds and QCA's Science Scheme of Work makes planning easy
- ◆ Sheets can be used on their own, integrated into other science schemes or used together as a comprehensive science scheme
- ◆ One book for KS1, three books for KS2
- ◆ Affordable photocopiable format

NEW for KS1!

Science for 5-7 Year Olds

This book contains over 70 attention-grabbing photocopiable sheets. Written in clear, simple language, with lots of helpful illustrations, they meet the needs of KS1 pupils. The accompanying teachers' notes tell you everything you need to know to help make science fun.

Activities include: investigating life cycles, growing plants, making a buzzer bleep, lighting a bulb, making an umbrella, floating objects, and many more.

The team of authors includes science specialists, primary school and special needs teachers.

Each book has over 60 clearly written, easy to follow, photocopiable worksheets.

Teachers' notes give background information, ideas for extensions, answers to pupil pages, resources needed and teaching/safety notes.

Other science titles

For Key Stage 2

How to be Brilliant at Electricity, Light & Sound

- 48 pages, photocopiable
- ISBN 1 897675 135

Practical activities to help children to acquire knowledge and understanding of electrical circuits, the everyday effects of light and how we see, and how sounds are made.

"... worth buying to support your science scheme and to help the busy non-specialist teacher." *Primary Science Review*

How to be Brilliant at Living Things

- 48 pages, photocopiable
- ISBN 1 897675 666

Activities to help your pupils learn about humans, plants and other living things and how they relate to their environment.

How to be Brilliant at Materials

- 48 pages, photocopiable
- ISBN 1 897675 127

Help children to acquire knowledge and understanding of the way materials are classified, how they can be changed and ways of separating different types of materials.

"... full of useful ideas, particularly to support structured practical activities ..." *Primary Science Review*

For Key Stage 1

How to Sparkle at Assessing Science

- 48 pages, photocopiable
- ISBN 1 897675 208

Assess and gather evidence of children's learning in science. Several sheets assess the development of science skills, helping children to structure their ideas, plans and findings more effectively, without being content specific. The remaining sheets let children demonstrate their grasp of science topics.

How to be Brilliant at Recording in Science

- 48 pages, photocopiable
- ISBN 1 897675 100

Generic writing frames covering all aspects of investigations from planning through to analysing results. Teacher sheets identify the potential learning objectives that the children could be steered towrds for each worksheet.

"This book is bound to move the learning experience forward." *Questions*

How to be Brilliant at Science Investigations

- 48 pages, photocopiable
- ISBN 1 897675 119

Help your pupils to acquire the experimental and investigative skills necessary to plan and carry out investigations. The photocopiable sheets provide opportunities for children to develop their observation skills, make measurements, plan and carry out investigations, and draw conclusions from the results.

How to Sparkle at Science Investigations

- 48 pages, photocopiable
- ISBN 1 897675 364

Using familiar contexts, these photocopiable sheets provide opportunities for children to develop their observation skills, make measurements, plan and carry out investigations, and draw conclusions from the results. The teachers' notes suggest ways in which the sheets can be built on or adapted to produce more investigations.

Brilliant Publications   sales: 01202 712910   website: www.brilliantpublications.co.uk

Printed in the United Kingdom
by Lightning Source UK Ltd.
103629UKS00001B/153-164